MW01114556

Vocabulary Learning Strategies and Foreign Language Acquisition

SECOND LANGUAGE ACQUISITION
Series Editor: Professor David Singleton, *Trinity College, Dublin, Ireland*

This series brings together titles dealing with a variety of aspects of language acquisition and processing in situations where a language or languages other than the native language is involved. Second language is thus interpreted in its broadest possible sense. The volumes included in the series all offer in their different ways, on the one hand, exposition and discussion of empirical findings and, on the other, some degree of theoretical reflection. In this latter connection, no particular theoretical stance is privileged in the series; nor is any relevant perspective – sociolinguistic, psycholinguistic, neurolinguistic, etc. – deemed out of place. The intended readership of the series includes final-year undergraduates working on second language acquisition projects, postgraduate students involved in second language acquisition research, and researchers and teachers in general whose interests include a second language acquisition component.

Other Books in the Series

For more details of these or any other of our publications, please contact:
Multilingual Matters, Frankfurt Lodge, Clevedon Hall,
Victoria Road, Clevedon, BS21 7HH, England
http://www.multilingual-matters.com

SECOND LANGUAGE ACQUISITION 27
Series Editor: David Singleton, *Trinity College, Dublin, Ireland*

Vocabulary Learning Strategies and Foreign Language Acquisition

Višnja Pavičić Takač

MULTILINGUAL MATTERS LTD
Clevedon • Buffalo • Toronto

Library of Congress Cataloging in Publication Data
Pavičić Takač, Višnja
Vocabulary Learning Strategies and Foreign Language Acquisition
Second Language Acquisition: 27
Includes bibliographical references and index.
1. Language and languages–Study and teaching. 2. Vocabulary–Study and teaching.
3. Second language acquisition. I. Title.
P53.9.P38 2008
418.007–dc22   2007040076

British Library Cataloguing in Publication Data
A catalogue entry for this book is available from the British Library.

ISBN-13: 978-1-84769-039-5 (hbk)
ISBN-13: 978-1-84769-038-8 (pbk)

Multilingual Matters Ltd
UK: Frankfurt Lodge, Clevedon Hall, Victoria Road, Clevedon BS21 7HH.
USA: UTP, 2250 Military Road, Tonawanda, NY 14150, USA.
Canada: UTP, 5201 Dufferin Street, North York, Ontario M3H 5T8, Canada.

The policy of Multilingual Matters/Channel View Publications is to use papers that
are natural, renewable and recyclable products, made from wood grown in
sustainable forests. In the manufacturing process of our books, and to further support
our policy, preference is given to printers that have FSC and PEFC Chain of Custody
certification. The FSC and/or PEFC logos will appear on those books where full
certification has been granted to the printer concerned.

Typeset by Datapage International Ltd.
Printed and bound in Great Britain by the Cromwell Press Ltd.

Contents

Introduction: An Outline of the Book

Second Language Acquisition,[1] as a field of scientific research and a foundation of contemporary language instruction, is still a relatively young discipline. Historically, second language instruction was either not grounded on any scientific theory (e.g. the Grammar-Translation Method), or was grounded on conclusions partly derived from valid linguistic theories and partly from general theories of learning (e.g. the influence of structural linguistics and behaviourism on the development of the audiolingual method). The Grammar-Translation Method was based on the fundamental assumption that learners will learn the target language simply by following the teaching method, whereas according to the audiolingual method the learner is conceived of as a passive recipient of the programme whose intervention would seriously interfere with the desirable automatic reaction. These theories received severe criticism from the new opposing theories, such as the interlanguage theory that views the learner as a creator of rules and errors as evidence of positive efforts by the learners to learn (Selinker, 1972). The new theories incited two general directions in SLA research: Rubin (1975) begins her work on raising awareness of learners' strategies of learning responsible for the language learning success, and Krashen (cf. 1981) proposes his influential theory which states that, for language acquisition to occur, learners need natural authentic communication, and not direct instruction. Due to this idea Krashen has often been recognised as the originator of the communicative approach to second language teaching. In addition to the above-mentioned approaches and methods, there is a host of other methods, often referred to as alternative, that have, in their own ways, influenced second language instruction. In general, language instruction today clearly reflects recognition and appreciation of the values and contributions of various methods and approaches.

In such an eclectic context, the cognitive theory of learning (i.e. a number of theories based on similar ideas and characterised by comparable conclusions) significantly influences the theory of second language learning and acquisition. Many theorists and researchers in the field of second language acquisition find that it is absolutely necessary to understand the interaction between language and cognition in order to explain the process of second language acquisition (e.g. Ellis, 2000; O'Malley & Chamot, 1996; Robinson, 2001; Skehan, 2000).

The ardent 'advocates' of the extreme cognitive approach entirely discard the behaviourist tenets; whereas the less radical cognitivists agree that the behaviourist theory is able to explain some aspects of learning. Gagné (1977, cited in Stern, 1986), for example, distinguishes several varieties of learning: learning intellectual skills, concepts and rules; learning problem solving or cognitive strategies; verbal information learning; motor skill learning; and the learning of attitudes. His conceptualisation of learning includes both behaviourist and cognitive principles and is reflected in his postulation that any concrete learning task, such as language learning, involves several or even all kinds of learning.

Zarevski (1994) finds it rather unrealistic to expect that one coherent theory can explain the whole complexity of learning. This is why the explanations within one theory range from the point of conflict to the point of interaction. The great strength of the cognitive theory lies in its capacity to explain the development of the competence to use the second language knowledge. This may serve as a basis for further developments of a more comprehensive theory that would be able to fully account for second language acquisition.

Due to the influence exerted by the cognitive theory of learning, the concept of language learning strategy or learner strategy referring to what learners do in order to make their learning manageable and efficient has become widely recognised in the field of second language acquisition.[2] An adequate explanation of how learning strategies contribute to the acquisition and attainment of the language has to account for a number of variables, from social and cultural learning context, covering varieties of factors influencing the use of strategies, to the language task.

This book focuses primarily upon vocabulary learning strategies. It aims at exploring what lies behind this phenomenon and examines both its linguistic and psychological aspect. Although the approach taken is rooted in the cognitive theory of learning (discussed in Chapter 2), we also look at the inherent linguistic features of lexical items and the complexity of lexical forms and relationships (Chapter 1). By doing so, we acknowledge the potential impact that these linguistic features may have on vocabulary acquisition, which the cognitive theory has been reputed to fail to do. Chapter 3 gives a critical review of previous research on vocabulary learning strategies. It is followed by an analysis of methods and instruments for assessing vocabulary learning strategies and of their advantages and drawbacks. Chapter 4 reports on three original studies on vocabulary learning strategies. The first one focuses on the problem of research methodology, i.e. designing an adequate instrument for measuring the use of vocabulary learning strategies. The second study explores the latent affect of instruction on the development of vocabulary learning strategies by investigating the relationship between vocabulary teaching strategies employed by teachers and vocabulary learning strategies selected by their learners. The third study examines the differences in the use of vocabulary learning strategies that may be attributed to the target language being learnt. This cross-linguistic study questions the universality and transferability of learning strategies and recognises the role that the social learning context may play in strategy use. Finally, implications for practice and further research are discussed.

Notes

1. Although I find the distinction between *learning* and *acquisition* (cf. Thatcher, 2000), and between *second* and *foreign language* useful and necessary, for reasons of general recognition and acceptance, the terms *second language* (L2) and *acquisition* will be used in this book, apart from instances where the distinction is a prerequisite for understanding the issues in question. *Second language* refers to both the language acquired in the environment where the target language is the language of communication and to the language acquired in the environment where the target language is not used for communication. The term implies that one language (first or native, L1) has already been acquired. In Chapter 4 of this book, the description of original research, the term *foreign language (FL)* will be used, because it refers to English learnt as a foreign language in an environment where another language (Croatian) is used for communication. The terms *acquisition* and *learning* will be used synonymously. Both terms are related to the processes of knowledge acquisition on the assumption that all learning is to some extent cognitively controlled. When it comes to vocabulary learning, the two processes are especially difficult to separate (Laufer, 1986). Thus, learning and acquisition will not be considered two different kinds of learning, but different degrees of knowledge acquisition.

2. According to Griffiths and Parr (2001), learning strategies have been implied by all methods and approaches to second language learning and teaching (e.g. the role of memory strategies in the Grammar-Translation Method, social strategies in the communicative approach, or affective strategies in suggestopaedia). Although they consider Krashen's theory an exception, it is his theory that Bialystok's (1979) concept of the monitoring strategy is based on. These examples emphasise the crucial role that language learning strategies should play in the language instruction programmes.

Chapter 1

Factors Affecting Vocabulary Learning and Acquisition

Despite the abundance of research on vocabulary acquisition that has been conducted by linguists, psychologists and theorists of L2 acquisition, there is still no generally accepted theory of vocabulary acquisition (for further discussion, see Meara, 1997). This fact may be partially attributed to the lack of cooperation or agreement among experts. On the one hand, psycholinguists have a particular interest in vocabulary development and exploration of the formal models of vocabulary acquisition, and ignore the L2 vocabulary literature *because* it is model-free. Applied linguists, on the other hand, are mainly concerned with the descriptive aspects of vocabulary and do not draw on existing psycho-linguistic models of bilingual lexicon even when this implies an immediate pedagogical significance. Differences in the research focus have caused the two fields to develop at different rates, which has led to an even larger gap between them. It is, therefore, extremely difficult to list all the significant factors and the ways in which they influence vocabulary acquisition. In this section, a selection of the factors most frequently discussed in the relevant literature is presented.

Linguistic Features of Lexical Items

When it comes to linguistic features of lexical items, several issues need to be taken into consideration. To begin with, there is the problem of defining a 'word'. Intuitively, vocabulary could be defined as a 'dictionary' or a set of words. This general view is reflected in the lexicographical approach to the traditional way of listing words in a dictionary. However, it is obvious that for linguistics and L2 acquisition theory this interpretation is far too simplistic and limited. Linguists' attempts to specify what speakers of a language traditionally regard as a 'word' have resulted in so many formally different definitions of this term that their number alone suggests the complexity of the problem.

Firstly, according to the orthographic definition, a 'word' is '... any sequence of letters (and a limited number of other characteristics such as hyphen and apostrophe) bounded on either side by a space or punctuation mark' (Carter, 1992: 4). Its flaw is not only its limitation to the written language, but the fact that it is formalistic, inconsistent and incomplete because it neglects differences in meaning and the issues of polysemy, homonymy, grammar functions, etc.

Secondly, based on semantics, a word can be defined as the smallest meaningful unit of language (Carter, 1992). As there is still no satisfactory definition of what 'meaning' is, i.e. what is the relationship between the linguistic sign and what it denotes outside the language, this definition is not reliable enough. Namely, some units of meaning consist of several words (e.g. *bus conductor*), for some the meaning cannot be determined without looking into their function in structuring and organising information (e.g. *if*, *but*), and certain 'integral' parts of words cannot stand on their own even if we know their meaning (e.g. the prefix '*re-*' in *retell*).

Thirdly, by the same token, the definition that restricts a word to a single stressed syllable allows for many exceptions: words like *if* and *but* do not have a stress, and *bus conductor* would be regarded as a single word in this view.

Next, Bloomfield's definition, according to which a word is a minimal free form, i.e. the smallest form that has a meaning when standing on its own (Škiljan, 1994), encompasses most of the categories and, without excluding further reduction of forms, provides a word with a degree of stability. Again, the problem of marginal cases arises and undermines every attempt to define a word in a formalistic way: firstly, items like *a* and *the* appear only in contextual relations to other words and secondly, idiomatic expressions, which consist of several orthographic words and cannot be reduced without radically changing their meaning (Carter, 1992).

Furthermore, McCarthy (1994) claims that a word, as a free meaningful unit of language, must contain at least one potentially freestanding morpheme. From this view a conditional definition of a word may be derived: a word is a combination of morphemes that comprise a firm unit suitable for the formation of higher level units (Škiljan, 1994). In addition, in Carter's view (1992), one of the greatest problems of defining a word, along with the above-mentioned constraints, is the fact that words have different forms that would *not* intuitively be regarded as different words. Moreover, words can have the same form with completely different and unconnected meanings.

Finally, by way of attempting to solve this problem, a neutral term *lexeme* or *lexical unit* has been introduced. It is an abstract unit that includes various orthographic, phonological, grammatical and semantic features of a 'word'. Thus, this term covers inflections, polysemy, as well as multi-word items with different degrees of fixedness, such as compounds, phrasal verbs, and idioms. The difference between holistic multi-word items and other kinds of strings (i.e. multi-word inflectional forms, such as verb phrases *are going* or *has been chosen*) may be determined by applying the following criteria: institutionalisation or lexicalisation (the degree to which a multi-word item is considered as being a unit by the language community), fixedness (the degree to which a multi-word item is frozen as a sequence of words) and non-compositionality (the degree to which a multi-word item cannot be interpreted on a word-by-word basis, but has a specialised unitary meaning) (cf. Moon, 1997: 44).

The second issue that needs to be discussed arises from the lack of an unambiguous and universally accepted definition of a word: vocabulary of any language consists of a wide range of lexical forms. Thus, many linguists and theorists of L2 acquisition agree that vocabulary is made up of a variety of forms, such as morphemes, both free and bound (e.g. *laugh*, or the prefix *un-*), their combinations, i.e. derivatives (e.g. *laughter*, *unbelievable*), compounds (e.g. *bus conductor*), idioms, i.e. units that cannot be reduced or changed, and whose meaning cannot be retrieved from individual meanings of their components (e.g. *to bite the dust*), and other fixed expressions, such as binomials and trinomials (e.g. *sick and tired*; *ready, willing and able*), catchphrases (e.g. *they don't make them like that any more*), prefabricated routines or prefabs (e.g. *if I were you*), greetings (e.g. *How do you do?*) and proverbs (e.g. *It never rains but it pours*). This list of formal categories indicates a tremendous heterogeneity and a wide range of lexical items, but is by no means complete and absolute, nor are the categories strictly demarcated: their overlap is inevitable. It is this aspect that places vocabulary on the boundaries between morphology, syntax and semantics.

The third issue takes into consideration the fact that lexical items can hardly be viewed in isolation from each other, for they enter, semantically speaking, into various relations. These include hyponyms (lexical items within the same semantic field, i.e. at content level), synonyms (two or more lexical items that have the same or nearly the same meaning but different form), antonyms (lexical items of opposite meanings) and homophones (lexical items that have the same form but different meanings).

Meaning can be studied by means of the so-called componential analysis, which is based on the assumption that the meaning of a lexical item can be broken down into a set of meaning components or semantic features. The meaning of a lexeme is determined by a number of distinctive semantic features, namely their absence (marked by '−'), presence (marked by '+') or irrelevance for the definition of a lexeme's meaning (marked by '±'). This approach shows which features of lexical items from the same semantic field overlap or differ, and is therefore suitable for the exploration of synonymy. A disadvantage of componential analysis is not only its failure to cover all meanings, but also the fact that it reduces the meaning components to binary oppositions that cannot always be precisely determined, and the fact that it may result in an indefinite list of a lexical item's relevant features.

The above-mentioned cases exemplify a paradigmatic relationship. This is the relationship between a lexeme and other lexemes that could be substituted for it in a sentence. A different type of relationship which lexemes enter into − called a syntagmatic relationship − is characterised by linear sequencing of lexemes. Such combinations of lexemes, however, are restricted. These restrictions (or 'collocations') determine which lexical units may be selected to form semantically acceptable combinations of two or more syntactically combined lexical units. Some collocations are entirely predictable (e.g. *blond* and *hair*); some lexical items have a wide range of collocations (e.g. *letter* collocates with *alphabet*, *box*, *post*, *write*, etc.), and some lexemes appear in so many different contexts that it is practically impossible to predict all of their collocations (e.g. verbs like *have* or *get*). To be noted is the fact that collocations differ from free associations of ideas: associations are highly individual, whereas collocations are lexical connections established in the same way by all speakers of a language. The study of collocations can be effective if it is conducted on large amounts of data, which is inevitably associated with corpus studies,[1] because collocations are not merely random combinations of lexical items, but are part of their meaning in the broadest sense of the word (Moon, 1997).

Finally, other factors influence the learning of a lexical item and make the acquisition of vocabulary difficult. According to Laufer (1997), the factors that affect the learnability of lexical items include pronounceability (phonological or suprasegmental features), orthography, length, morphology, including both inflectional and derivational complexity that increase the vocabulary learning load, similarity of lexical forms (e.g. synforms,[2] homonyms), grammar, i.e. part of speech, and semantic features (e.g. abstractness, specificity and register restriction, idiomaticity and multiple meaning). Table 1.1 gives an overview of the intralexical factors and their effect on vocabulary learning (facilitating factors,

Table 1.1 Intralexical factors that affect vocabulary learning (Laufer, 1997: 154)

Facilitating factors	Difficulty-inducing factors	Factors with no clear effect
Familiar phonemes	Presence of foreign phonemes	
Phonotactic regularity	Phonotactic irregularity	
Fixed stress	Variable stress and vowel change	
Consistency of sound–script relationship	Incongruency in sound–script relationship	
		Word length
Inflexional regularity	Inflexional complexity	
Derivational regularity	Derivational complexity	
Morphological transparency	Deceptive morphological transparency	
	Synformy	
		Part of speech
		Concreteness/abstractness
Generality	Specificity	
Register neutrality	Register restrictions	
	Idiomaticity	
One form for one meaning	One form with several meanings	

difficulty-inducing factors and factors with no clear effect) (Laufer, 1997: 154).

The Influence of First and Other Languages

L2 vocabulary acquisition is different from L1 vocabulary acquisition because an L2 learner has already developed conceptual and semantic systems linked to the L1. This is why L2 acquisition, at least in its initial stages, often involves a mapping of the new lexical form onto an already existing conceptual meaning or translational equivalent in L1. The role of L1 in this process varies depending on the degree of equivalency between languages: although in some cases it may facilitate the acquisition or use of L2 lexical items, in others it will create an obstacle. This may occur in the process of acquisition, in recalling and using previously learnt lexical items, or in attempts of constructing a complex lexical item that has not been learnt as a unit. By making cross-linguistic comparisons (i.e. by contrastive analysis) one can often predict difficulties caused by interference of the L1 that learners may encounter when learning the target language. Namely, the learner's approach to L2 learning is based on an 'equivalence hypothesis': 'the learner tends to assume that the system of L2 is more or less the same as in his L1 until he has discovered that it is not' (Ringbom, 1987: 135). The learner's readiness to transfer may also be influenced by his perceptions of linguistic and cultural distance. Forming a kind of equivalence hypothesis enables learners to learn an L2 without having to go all the way back to learning how to categorise the world. However, equivalence hypothesis may fail and lead to erroneous conclusions because of the following reasons (Swan, 1997):

- lexical units in two languages are not exact equivalents (i.e. there is more than one translation);
- equivalent lexical units in related languages have different permissible grammatical contexts;
- equivalents belong to different word classes;
- equivalents are false friends;
- there are no equivalents at all.

Coping with these problems may be overwhelming, and the learners tend to avoid such 'difficult' lexical items, especially if there is a semantic void in the L1. A possible explanation is that in such cases there is no foundation on which L2 knowledge may be built (Gass, 1989).

Finally, the L2 learner, unlike the child acquiring its L1, cannot significantly expand his or her vocabulary solely through exposure to the language input. The exposure to L2 input is often limited to the classroom context. The input may be increased by reading (cf. Ellis, 1997) or listening (Rivers, 1981) in the target language. But these activities, although undoubtedly useful, do not guarantee the development of rich vocabulary. Similarly, formal teaching of vocabulary has its limitations, for, as Rivers (1981: 463) claims, 'vocabulary cannot be taught'.

The Incremental Nature of Vocabulary Acquisition

Knowledge of an L2 lexical item consists of several components. Generally, it is characterised by several dimensions of word knowledge (i.e. phonological and orthographic, morphological, syntactic and semantic) and by knowledge of conceptual foundations that determine the position of the lexical item in our conceptual system. Finally, it inevitably includes the ability of productive use, i.e. efficient retrieval of the lexical item for active use.

Ideally, knowledge of a lexical item would include all of the above-mentioned dimensions and would be reflected in the ability to react in the manner of an educated native speaker. However, knowledge of a lexical item is not an 'all-or-nothing' proposition; it is rather to be conceived of as a continuum of knowledge at whose ends, according to some theoreticians, the receptive and productive knowledge is placed. It can be concluded that even partial knowledge represents a degree of knowing a lexical item. The initial degree is elementary knowledge, such as the visual recognition of a lexical item in a context that still does not enable a learner to produce it. Higher degrees of knowledge, close to productive knowledge, would suggest, for example, knowledge of multiple meanings of a polysemous lexical item or its collocations, etc. Whereas interpretation requires only as much information as is necessary to distinguish a lexical item from all other possibilities, production requires more information, which may even include the aid of an adequate stimulus (e.g. context) (Melka, 1997).

The Role of Memory in Vocabulary Learning and Acquisition

The role of memory[3] is crucial in any kind of learning and vocabulary learning is no exception. According to the above-described continuum, learning of lexical items is not linear. Learners, without fail, forget some components of knowledge. In both long-term and short-term memory forgetting takes place in a similar way. When obtaining new information, most of it is forgotten immediately, after which the process of forgetting slows down. On the basis of available research results, Thornbury (2002) has compiled a list of principles that facilitate the transfer of the learning material into the long-term memory. These include multiple encounters with a lexical item, preferably at spaced intervals, retrieval and use of lexical items, cognitive depth (cf. Schneider *et al.*, 2002), affective depth, personalisation, imaging, use of mnemonics[4] and conscious attention that is necessary to remember a lexical item. A proper understanding of the role memory plays in vocabulary acquisition has an immediate practical value: as lexical knowledge is more prone to attrition than other linguistic aspects (Schmitt, 2000), the learning and teaching of vocabulary needs to be planned following the above mentioned principles if it is to be efficient.

The Organisation and Development of the Second Language Mental Lexicon

L2 vocabulary development is also influenced by the organisation of the mental lexicon. The mental lexicon is 'a memory system in which a vast number of words, accumulated in the course of time, has been stored' (Hulstijn, 2000: 210). This system is seen to be organised and structured, because it is the only possible explanation for the fact that people can, at an astonishing rate, in a vast quantity of lexical items stored in the memory, recognise and retrieve the lexical item they need to express what they want. Human memory is very flexible and it can 'process' a large quantity of data, but only if it is systematically organised.

It is not easy to gather the data on the organisation and functioning of the mental lexicon. Some answers can be found by studying various speakers' behaviour, such as tip-of-the-tongue phenomena, slips of the tongue and problems manifested by people who suffer from aphasia (Aitchison, 1990) or by analysing communication strategies used by L2 learners (Ridley, 1997). It is understandable, therefore, that many conclusions about the development and organisation of the mental lexicon are based on assumptions. Nevertheless, such studies have yielded results that significantly contribute to modelling the mental lexicon.[5] Research on the L2 mental lexicon is further complicated by the presence of at least one more language. In addition to the organisation and development of the L2 mental lexicon, these studies deal with similarities and differences between the L1 and L2 mental lexicon and the degree of separation or integration of the two systems.

The term *mental lexicon* or *mental dictionary* is reminiscent of a traditional printed book dictionary only because it refers to a collection of lexical items. But, a printed dictionary is necessarily static, limited and prone to become outdated, whilst the mental lexicon encompasses a multitude of features suggesting a more complex yet far more efficient organisation. Aitchison (1990) lists additional differences between the mental lexicon and a book dictionary.

The mental lexicon can partially be organised according to initial sounds, but the order will not be strictly alphabetical as in book dictionaries. Other features of a lexical item's structure, such as suffixes or stress, may also play a role in its placement in the mind. Furthermore, words in the mind seem to be connected into semantic networks, and the strongest links, as shown by association tests, are coordination and collocation. Moreover, the mental lexicon is characterised by fluidity and flexibility (Aitchison, 1990: 12). These characteristics are reflected in the unlimited human creativity in applying the knowledge in new ways and interpreting new situations in light of previous knowledge. But the amount and the range of information on every single 'entry' provided by the mental lexicon (such as information on collocation, meanings in relation to other words, frequency of usage, syntactic patterns a word may slot into, etc.) must be held as the greatest difference between the mental lexicon and the dictionary-book. Also, the mental lexicon offers multiple access to information; processes of word recognition and word production activate more words than necessary, only to make a final selection and suppress the 'unnecessary' information.

On the basis of the above considerations it is assumed that the place of a word in the mental lexicon should be represented by a three-dimensional model 'with phonological nets crossing orthographic ones and criss-crossing semantic and encyclopaedic nets' (McCarthy, 1994: 41). However, the links between individual nets are very fragile and can 'break'. This is manifested in such cases when a speaker cannot produce the sound of the word although he/she has produced it before, knows that it exists and what it means, and can even give many descriptive details about it. This situation, in addition to the fact that a speaker of a language can understand novel forms, is often taken as empirical evidence supporting the existence of the dichotomy between receptive and productive vocabulary.[6] Speakers of a language intuitively support this view and assume that receptive vocabulary is much larger than productive vocabulary, and that receptive vocabulary precedes productive vocabulary. The current literature, however, does not offer an adequate definition of the two notions, and the distinction has been criticised as being too simplistic in that it implies the idea of the mental lexicon as a static unit consisting of two separate compartments. Melka (1997) has concluded from the review of a number of studies that there are two directions in understanding the dichotomy between receptive and productive vocabulary. On the one hand, reception is thought to precede production and the distance between the two asymmetric notions is fairly large. Moreover, reception and production are two different processes dependent on different mental processes. An opposing view is that reception may precede production, but the gap between the two notions is not that significant and it varies and shifts. The abovementioned contrasting views of reception and production have led to different estimates of receptive and productive vocabularies (cf. Melka, 1997). One group of researchers estimates the receptive vocabulary to be double the size of productive vocabulary, another that the distance between reception and production, although constantly present, diminishes with the development of knowledge, and a third group does not find the gap that significant at all. Although it is impossible to reach a definite conclusion, primarily because of different ways of testing and interpreting results, it is plausible to suppose that the 'truth may lie between the second and the third possibilities', says Melka (1997: 93). A further suggestion put forward by the same scholar is that the notions of receptive and productive vocabularies should be replaced by other notions, such as *familiarity* and degrees or continuum of knowledge. Namely, there are different stages of familiarity with a lexical item that enables one to recognise it when its production is still impossible. These stages bring us closer to the border of reception and production and to the point where reception finishes and production starts, if only partially. The mental lexicon is seen as 'a mixed system which has found a workable compromise between the requirements of production and those of comprehension' (Aitchison, 1990: 193).[7]

Although research on human capacity to acquire, store and use vocabulary has been conducted to a large extent on L1, these findings may be a source of useful information for more efficient learning and teaching of second or foreign languages as well. This is not to suggest – as McCarthy (1994) points out – that the processes of storing, memorising and recalling are identical in L1 and L2. Similarities exist but may have different manifestations. An example of this is the fact that the dynamic characteristic of the mental lexicon becomes more prominent in L2 learning; not only are new lexical items constantly added, but the information on existing ones is expanded and completed. Dynamism is also reflected in the concept of spreading activation (Hulstijn, 2000). For example, two lexical items can be stored without any interconnection. After that, they can be linked via some formal or semantic features, with other types of links being added later on. These links are characterised by different degrees of strength, which also varies; it can increase or diminish in the course of time. Moreover, memory strategies, such as the Keyword Method, facilitate the formation of such links.

The debate on similarities and differences between L1 lexicon and L2 lexicon(s) can be summarised into four basic hypotheses as follows (Hulstijn, 2000):

(1) the extended system hypothesis: L1 words and L2 words are stored in a single store);
(2) the dual system hypothesis: words are stored in separate stores;
(3) the tripartite hypothesis: similar words (e.g. cognates) are stored in a common store, and language-specific words are stored in separate stores;
(4) the subset hypothesis: L1 words and L2 words are stored in two relatively separated subsets, but both subsets are stored in a common store.

It is claimed by many that for L2 learners networks of semantic associations are not the most frequent way of word association as is the case in the native language: more often L2 learners connect words on the basis of their phonological similarity. Meara (1984) concludes on the basis of his research that techniques for word storage and handling may depend on the language, i.e. that the L2 mental lexicon is considerably different from that of the native speaker. Consequently, says Meara, learners use strategies inadequate for the given language, which can account for some difficulties in L2 learning. Swan's approach to this issue is somewhat different. He claims that one should not conclude that there are '... generalisable, significant qualitative differences between the L2 mental lexicon and the L1 mental lexicon for all language learners' (Swan, 1997: 175). The above-mentioned difficulties in L2 learning may as well be attributed to other factors. According to Singleton (1999), the conclusion that the activation of the mental lexicon is primarily phonologically conditioned has been made on the basis of the nature of the research design.[8] The implication is that in L2 learning attending to form precedes attending to meaning.[9] There is, however, a body of research findings suggesting other possible explanations. For example, results of the study conducted by O'Gorman (1996) supply evidence in favour of semantic links with prompts. Worth noting in this context is the finding of Henning (1973) who explored the parameters of lexical coding in memory. Focusing his research on two parameters, that of semantic and that of acoustic grouping, Henning attempted to answer the question whether L2 learners code vocabulary in the memory in phonological or semantic clusters, and whether there is a correlation between learners' proficiency and the type of coding. The results indicated that learners do code vocabulary in acoustic and semantic clusters. Namely, low-proficiency learners registered vocabulary by phonological rather than semantic similarities, whereas high-proficiency learners demonstrated the reverse: they relied more on meaning than sound. One can therefore assume that formal processing is equally important in L1 and L2 mental lexicons, particularly in the initial stages of learning, whilst semantic processing takes over in the advanced stages of linguistic development. The Trinity College Dublin Modern Languages Research Project (cf. Ridley, 1997; Singleton, 1999) has shown concretely that lexical interconnections and operational procedures were semanticopragmatic in nature (at least in the tests used in the studies). Moreover, their findings seem to refute the idea that L1 and L2 mental lexicons are separate entities, but do not suggest their total integration either. Singleton (1999) assumes that the relationship between the two lexicons corresponds to the above-mentioned subset hypothesis: although stored separately, the L1 and L2 lexicons communicate either via direct links between L1 and L2 lexical nodes, or via a common conceptual store (or both). What is implied in the above discussion – and what is of immediate relevance for the subject of this book – is that the lexicosemantical relationship, i.e. the relationship between an L1 and an L2 word in the mental lexicon, is likely to vary from individual to individual. What this suggests is that organisational resources (such as L1 and L2 connections) available in the mental lexicon are used by every individual in a different way, depending on the way the word has been acquired, on the level of the word's acquisition, and on the perception of formal and/or semantic similarity between the L1 and L2 word. Obviously, a balance must be struck between the aspiration to determine universalities in L2 acquisition and the fact that there are individual differences influencing all aspects of L2 learning and teaching.

A number of studies, reported in Gass (1989), seem to associate the organisation of the mental lexicon with the concept of prototypes. The theory of lexical prototypes reflects the idea that some concepts are central and more prominent, or 'best-fit members of a conceptual category' (Gass, 1989: 101). Other members of the given conceptual category are peripheral. For example, given the field of 'vehicle', most native speakers would mention 'car' as the prototypical member of the category, followed by items such as 'boat, scooter, tricycle, horse, skis' (McCarthy, 1994). Gass (1989) also points to a significant body of research showing the prototypes to be the foundation for L2 vocabulary development: learners more readily learn the prototypical meanings of lexical items, whereas non-prototypical meanings are learnt later.

Furthermore, errors often occur in the area of non-prototypicality, i.e. where L1 meanings do not overlap with L2 meanings.

The Source of Vocabulary (Exposure to Linguistic Input)

Research on L1 vocabulary acquisition has shown that the primary source of vocabulary for native speakers is a wide range of contexts that enable them to experiment and to confirm, expand or narrow down the lexical nets (Carter, 1992). Naturally, this process is not based on explicit formal instruction, but on incidental learning from large amounts of language input. When it comes to learning an L2, however, the answer is not that simple. Although some research results have confirmed the assumption that L2 vocabulary can also be acquired through exposure to various contexts (such as reading, see Sternberg, 1987), these conclusions cannot be interpreted without taking into consideration the factors that directly affect the efficiency of the process. Clearly, the role of the context in initial stages of vocabulary learning is relatively negligible. The success of contextual inferencing will depend on the learner's proficiency level, i.e. on the various categories of knowledge (linguistic knowledge, world knowledge and strategic knowledge) that the learner needs to apply (Nagy, 1997).

Beginners do not have enough linguistic knowledge, so they have to make deliberate attempts at learning lexical items often connected to a synonym, definition, translation into L1, or an illustration. A significant amount of vocabulary can be successfully learnt through the often criticised rote learning (Carter, 1992). Still, vocabulary acquisition is not merely a mental collection of individual lexical items with a 1:1 correspondence to L1 lexical items. As has already been mentioned, familiarity with a lexical item includes more than knowing its semantic aspect. Vocabulary learning is the acquisition of memorised sequences of lexical items that serve as a pattern on the basis of which the learner creates new sequences. The main task is to discover the patterns in the language, starting from phonological categories, phonotactic sequences (i.e. allowable arrangement of phonemes), and morphemes, to collocations and lexical phrases, and their analysis into meaningful units or chunks (which are units of memory organisation). This implies that language production is based on assembling ready-made chunks suitable for particular situations, and that language comprehension relies on the ability to predict the pattern that will appear in a given situation. Although it might appear illogical at first sight, it is the ability to use conventionalised and predictable language sequences that brings an L2 learner closer to the native speaker. Namely, 'native speakers do *not* exercise the creative potential of syntactic rules of a generative grammar' (Ellis, 1997: 129), it is the use of idiomatic, frequent and familiar units that reflects a native-like competence. Therefore, the task of the L2 learner is to acquire lexical sequences (collocations, phrases and idioms), as well as sequences within lexical units. A precondition for an automatic analysis of such information is sufficient exposure to language input or explicit teaching and awareness raising (Ellis, 1997).

An important source of vocabulary in L2 learning is a wide range of contexts. Learners can learn lexical items if they are exposed to sufficient amounts of comprehensible input. Nagy (1997) claims that an average learner can learn to recognise up to 1000 words a year from written materials. As has already been stated, the role of the context in initial stages of learning is limited, but its significance grows as the learner's knowledge expands. An ideal source for learning L2 vocabulary from context is reading (Ellis, 1997). Low-frequency lexical items (the ones that are characteristic of individuals with a wide vocabulary) occur more frequently in written than in spoken language. Besides, the learner has more time at his or her disposal for analysis, hypothesis testing and inferencing if working on a written text. Context-based inferencing contributes to the knowledge of morphological rules, collocations, additional meanings (for it is the context that determines the meaning of a lexical unit), etc. However, mere exposure during reading does not guarantee a rapid vocabulary growth. In order to accelerate the process, the learner must have critical strategic knowledge that will enable him or her to turn the incidental learning into an explicit learning process.

Individual Learner Differences

Vocabulary learning strategies play an important role in vocabulary learning. Their significance is reflected practically in all the factors discussed so far. Vocabulary learning strategies activate explicit learning that entails many aspects, such as making conscious efforts to notice new lexical items, selective attending, context-based inferencing and storing into long-term memory (Ellis, 1994). However, the influence of other factors that account for individual learner differences, such as the affective ones (motivation, attitudes towards vocabulary learning, fear of failure) or the language learning aptitude, should not be neglected. This will be addressed in more detail in Chapter 2.

The Role of the Teacher and Vocabulary Teaching Strategies

Finally, in the discussion of the factors influencing vocabulary learning, we come to the question that is of great significance in the framework of formal L2 instruction, namely that of the teacher and vocabulary teaching strategies. A look at the teaching practices in the past suggests that the status of formal vocabulary teaching has always been influenced by current trends in linguistic and psycholinguistic research. The naturalistic approach to language teaching, for example, favoured implicit incidental vocabulary learning. The emphasis was on guessing the meaning from context and using monolingual dictionaries, whereas defining and translating lexical items were to be avoided. However, a closer look at the effects of exposure to a variety of contexts – generally considered as extremely important in vocabulary acquisition – revealed that inferring word meaning is no easy matter. A precondition for successful inferencing is a sufficient level of knowledge and inference skills. However, even if this precondition is met, inferring word meaning may still result in incorrect guessing, and such errors may be difficult to rectify. Although having inference skills may contribute to vocabulary growth, rich vocabulary is not necessarily a consequence of having inference skills. All in all, implicit incidental learning seems to be a slow and inefficient process which does not necessarily imply long-term retention (Sökmen, 1997).

It has become apparent, on the basis of the above-mentioned arguments, to all subjects involved in the processes of language teaching and learning, that vocabulary acquisition cannot rely on implicit incidental learning but needs to be controlled. The advocates of this view – not disputing the significance of acquiring grammatical – syntactical structures or the role of the context – have begun to insist on more intensive, explicit vocabulary teaching from the very beginning of any language learning programme (Judd, 1978). Explicit vocabulary teaching would ensure that lexical development in the target language follows a systematic and logical path, thus avoiding uncontrolled accumulation of sporadic lexical items. However, the contribution and effect of explicit vocabulary teaching on vocabulary acquisition is still under dispute. Learners do not learn everything that teachers teach. Lewis (2000b) describes teaching as being linear and systematic, but it is wrong to conceive of learning as being the same. The contemporary approach to vocabulary teaching, one concludes, recognises the importance of both implicit and explicit teaching, taking into account the results of scientific research, with the aim to increase the efficiency of teaching and learning of target language vocabulary.[10]

In vocabulary teaching, teachers can apply a host of strategies and activities.[11] According to Hatch and Brown (2000: 401), teaching strategies refer to everything teachers do or should do in order to help their learners learn. Which teaching strategy a teacher will employ depends on the time available, the content (i.e. the component of knowledge learners are to acquire), as well as on its value for the learner (i.e. which learning strategy he or she can learn or apply). Teaching strategies are also dependent on specific principles and in correlation with other factors influencing vocabulary acquisition discussed earlier in this chapter. A distinction is made between planned and unplanned vocabulary teaching strategies (Seal, 1991). Unplanned teaching strategies relate to teachers' spontaneous reactions with the aim to help learners when the need arises, in which case teachers improvise. Seal suggests *The three C's*, a three-step procedure where the teacher (1) conveys the meaning, (2) checks meaning by, for example, asking questions and (3) consolidates the meaning in learners' memory by, for example, relating it to the context or personal experience.

Planned vocabulary teaching refers to deliberate, explicit, clearly defined and directed vocabulary teaching. It encompasses the use of teaching strategies, i.e. ways in which teachers introduce and present the meaning and form of new lexical items, encourage learners to review and practice, i.e. recycle what is known, and monitor and evaluate the level of acquisition of various components of lexical knowledge. Such teaching presupposes dedicating a certain amount of time to dealing with vocabulary, involving 'exploration' of the different aspects of lexical knowledge, as well as inducing learners to actively process lexical items (cf. Nation, 2001). A review of the literature (Hatch & Brown, 2000; Nation, 2001; Sökmen, 1997; Thornbury, 2002) has yielded a comprehensive list of teaching strategies that fall into two major categories: (1) presentation of meaning and form of new lexical items and (2) review and consolidation (recycling and practising) of presented lexical items. In the following subsections we turn to a more detailed exploration of each of the two categories.

Presentation of new lexical items

Under the presentation of new lexical items one understands the teaching of preselected lexical items in the planned stage of a lesson. Learners are mostly passive recipients of linguistic facts, although some procedures may involve learners' active participation. The teacher presents both the meaning and form of the lexical item, which may occur in either order. The meaning of lexical items can be presented verbally or non-verbally. The most frequently mentioned ways of presentation are the following:

- *Connecting an L2 item with its equivalent in L1.* This teaching strategy is mostly used when checking comprehension, but can also be used when it is necessary to point out the similarities or differences between L2 and L1, especially when these are likely to cause errors (e.g. false pairs, connotations or sociolinguistic rules affecting word choice, etc.).
- *Defining the meaning.* Definitions can take many forms: synonym, antonym, analytic definition (*X is a Y which*), taxonomic definition (*Autumn is a season*), giving examples (*Furniture – something like a chair, sofa, etc.*) or the reverse, giving the superordinate term (*A rose is a flower*), describing the function (*Pen – use it to write*), grammatical definition (*worse – comparison of bad*), definition by connection (*danger – lives have not been protected*), definition by classification (*Family – a group of people*), and the so-called full definition, the one resembling word definitions in monolingual dictionaries. Definitions should be simple and clear and supplemented with other procedures with the view to lexical development and long-term retention of lexical items.
- *Presentation through context.* The teacher creates a situation (a sort of a scenario) in which he or she clearly contextualises the lexical item. The context can be given in one sentence only, but the teacher can also give several sentences in which the word appears. Learners then guess the meaning on the basis of the cumulative effect of the sentences.
- *Directly connecting the meaning to real objects or phenomena.* This strategy is widely used with beginners or young learners. It includes procedures such as demonstration, realia and visual aids, which at the same time serve as cues for remembering lexical items. These actions are even more effective if supplemented by, for example, a verbal definition, not only because it reduces the possibility of incorrect guessing, but also because it results in 'dual encoding', i.e. linguistic and visual storing of information (Nation, 2001).
- *Active involvement of learners in presentation.* The teacher encourages learners to discover the word's meaning from its parts or by elicitation: for example, the teacher shows a picture and invites

learners to supply a word, or the teacher gives the word but invites learners to give its definition or synonym. Worth adding here is personalisation, because it enhances memory, as has already been noted earlier in this chapter.

Furthermore, in order to establish a connection between meaning and form learners need to be stimulated to attend to the orthographic and phonological form of the word as well. The following are some of the ways in which the form can be presented:

- *Oral drill.* The teacher pronounces the word several times, learners listen. Learners repeat the word aloud (chorally or individually), and then learners individually pronounce the word to themselves (in low tones).
- *Phonetic transcription and graphic presentation* (of the stressed syllable, for example).
- *Presentation of the graphic form* (by writing the word on the board, underlining it or highlighting it in the text).
- *Encouraging learners to try and spell the word.*

Review and consolidation of lexical items

The second category of vocabulary teaching strategies refers to those procedures whose aim is to get learners to review lexical items, for this review is necessary, as has been stated on several occasions so far, to consolidate them in long-term memory. According to the principle labelled as 'expanded rehearsal' (see Schmitt, 2000), it is necessary to review the material immediately after initial learning and then at gradually increasing intervals (e.g. 5–10 minutes after learning, then 24 hours later, a week later, a month later and finally 6 months later). The teacher's task is to provide learners with opportunities for practising and connecting words in various ways and to stimulate them to retrieve words from memory and use them for all language skills. Principles of memorising words, discussed in one of the above sections, may serve as guidelines in planning and selecting tasks and activities at this stage of vocabulary teaching. The activities most frequently mentioned in the literature are the following:

- *Mechanical repetition of words.* Although deep level processing is more effective in the long run, loud repetition may also contribute to memorisation of a word.
- *Copying words.* If accompanied, for example, by loud repetition or visualisation of its meaning, copying can aid memory. If learners

copy words onto word cards, other possibilities of revision activities present themselves.

- *Word manipulation.* This includes examples of tasks such as matching words and their definitions, grouping words, finding the odd one out, etc.

- *Integrating new words with the already known.* Activating linguistic pre-knowledge and knowledge of the world creates a link between new words and already known words. In the process of creating the links, new words become more meaningful and organised, and thus easier to learn. This can be achieved in various ways, as for example by semantic elaboration.

- *Semantic elaboration.* It facilitates the creation of links and semantic networks, as well as deep level of processing. According to Sökmen (1997), the following are procedures based on semantic elaboration: semantic feature analysis (e.g. a componential analysis); semantic mapping, which also serves as a visual reminder of links between words; ordering or classifying words, which helps learners to organise and distinguish differences in meaning between words; pictorial schemata, such as grids or diagrams, which emphasise distinctive features and require learners to deeply process words by organising words and making their meanings visual and concrete. These techniques are also suitable for presenting and revising collocations.

- *Creating mental images* by drawing diagrams, illustrations of meaning etc.

- *Personalisation.* Personalisation makes the learning material psychologically 'real'. It can be achieved by giving personal examples, i.e. by relating a word to real events or personal experience, etc.

- *Tasks for word identification.* The aim of these tasks is to get learners to pay attention to specific lexical items and to recognise their form. Concrete examples are finding words in a text, working on a 'word snake' puzzle, solving anagrams, etc.

- *Tasks for recalling words from memory.* Activating knowledge, i.e. an attempt to recall a word's meaning with the help of the given form or vice versa, by recalling the form on the basis of given meaning, and thereby enhancing memory. Therefore, the teacher should deliberately encourage recall at spaced intervals. This task may be realised through a number of activities: acting the word out, replacing the word with its synonym or antonym, giving a definition, translation, cross-word puzzles, etc. Also, reading and listening activities stimulate word identification.

- *Tasks for expansion of lexical knowledge.* These are concerned with providing additional information on lexical items in order to cover as many components of lexical knowledge as possible. The activities that seem worthwhile in this respect are analysis of word formation, analysis of grammar categories and forms, highlighting collocations, etc.
- *Productive use of words.* By using words in a meaningful context learners create mental links. Activities that promote productive use of vocabulary include the following: completing sentences or texts, with words offered or not, using words in sentences, conversations, stories, etc.; various games (e.g. *Hangman, I spy, Bingo*). All speaking and writing activities by definition include productive use of vocabulary.
- *Multiple encounters with the word.* All above-listed activities can offer learners opportunities to encounter words many times and in different contexts. A variety of tasks and multiple encounters of a word ensure a more systematic coverage of various aspects of lexical knowledge and enable learners to build up an adequate lexical knowledge and consolidate it in long-term memory.

When planning and teaching a vocabulary lesson, in addition to the tasks and objectives discussed above, one must take into consideration general teaching strategies, principles of planning and organising a lesson, and other relevant components of the teaching process. Not unlike in other areas of L2 teaching, in vocabulary teaching the teacher continuously monitors comprehension and production, corrects errors, directs, evaluates, tests, encourages and rewards his or her learners. It is the teacher's mission to motivate learners and develop their interest in expanding their lexical knowledge. Related to this is the reason why teachers should make every effort to ensure a continuous and systematic revision and assessment in vocabulary and to insist on lexical richness. This awareness of the need for constant lexical development is especially important at advanced levels in order to prevent learners from using the avoidance strategy and from opting for semantic extension (Laufer, 1991). Formal L2 vocabulary instruction should be based on a variety of teaching techniques and activities in order to cater for individual learning styles and to break the classroom routines. It is of extreme importance to encourage learners' active participation in vocabulary learning and cooperation with their peers and the teacher. Also, learners need to be supported in their own discovery of lexical items, in finding ways of expanding their lexical knowledge (by, for example, giving them confidence in using a dictionary), and in a systematic and continuous expansion of vocabulary outside the classroom as well (by emphasising the need for taking notes, recycling, the importance of exposure to language input through reading or the media, etc.). It is in this latter context that vocabulary learning strategies become prominent. Although vocabulary learning strategies are embedded in practically all objectives and principles of L2 vocabulary teaching, it is recommended – on the basis of research findings – that elements of explicit strategy training be included. At any rate, learners need to be encouraged to discover new and develop the existing vocabulary learning strategies in order to be able to deal with lexical items on their own and outside the classroom.

Conclusion

To conclude, one has to admit that achieving the goals of L2 vocabulary instruction is no easy matter. Even a well planned vocabulary lesson based on contemporary pedagogical principles cannot guarantee that learners will acquire the vocabulary that is taught. Learning vocabulary through formal instruction is a complex process influenced by a number of factors: the teacher's approach to vocabulary teaching (i.e. vocabulary teaching strategies) and his or her understanding of the key notions in vocabulary acquisition, the effort invested by learners in vocabulary learning (i.e. vocabulary learning strategies) as well as their readiness to take responsibility for their own learning, and, finally, the interaction of all the factors discussed in this chapter.

Notes

1. For more on corpora see McCarthy and Carter (1997).
2. Laufer (1997) lists 10 different categories of synforms, each representing a different type of similarity between the target lexical item and the error produced by L2 learners.
3. cf. Stevick (1996).
4. see Chapter 3.
5. For an extensive review of the most frequently quoted models of the L1 mental lexicon, see Singleton (1999).
6. In the literature there is a host of different terms used, not necessarily synonymously, to refer to receptive and productive vocabulary, the most frequent being the following: active versus passive; comprehension versus production; understanding versus speaking, recognitional vocabulary versus actual or possible use.
7. For the summary of the organisation requirements of the mental lexicon see Aitchison (1990: 198–199).

8. Singleton (1999) criticises the experiments within the Birkbeck Vocabulary Project. The test contained rare (or unfamiliar) lexical items, i.e. items for which there were no previously established connections of different kinds.
9. Hatch and Brown (2000) cite Brown and Payne's work on learners' approach to vocabulary learning, which supports this inference. See also Chapter 3.
10. This principle is embedded in the lexical approach (cf. the works of Lewis, 1998; 2000a), which is based on applied linguistics. The fundamental assumption of this approach is that vocabulary and grammar are not strictly separated, because language consists of an indefinite number of language patterns.
11. A variety of practical resource books for teachers containing descriptions of activities for explicit vocabulary teaching are available (e.g. Allen, 1983; Gairns & Redman, 1986; Lewis, 1998; Morgan & Rinvolucri, 1986; Thornbury, 2002). These are primarily intended for teaching English as L2, but the activities can be adapted to teaching other languages as well.

Chapter 2

Theoretical Anchorage

This chapter concerns itself with the theoretical background to the phenomenon of learning strategies. A precondition for understanding vocabulary learning strategies is a clear idea of what language learning strategies are in general. Therefore, this chapter discusses the role of general language learning strategies in cognitive theory and other relevant L2 acquisition theories and models. The second part of the chapter explores the problem of establishing criteria for defining the concept of language learning strategies, their features and classifications.

The Cognitive Theory of Learning

We first turn to the cognitive theory of learning for what seems an obvious reason: unlike linguistic theories of L2 acquisition, the cognitive theory recognises learning strategies as one of the significant cognitive processes in L2 acquisition.

Generally speaking, the cognitive theory of learning, which is largely based on the theory of human information processing, deals with mental processes involved in learning. This mainly refers to three fundamental cognitive aspects of learning: how knowledge is developed, how knowledge becomes automatic and how new knowledge is integrated into an existing cognitive system of the learner.

Emphasis is placed on 'meaningful learning', i.e. learning with understanding which is not manifested in behaviour, but which can be described as 'a clearly articulated and precisely differentiated conscious experience that emerges when potentially meaningful signs, symbols, concepts, or propositions are related to and incorporated within a given individual's cognitive structure' (Ausubel, 1967: 10).

Findings of research conducted in the domains of cognitive psychology and psycholinguistics had reverberations in the area of L2 acquisition. Research within the latter field has attempted to find, among other things, answers to questions concerning the nature of cognitive skills, namely the ways in which they affect L2 acquisition and learning, and the possible role of formal instruction. Because cognitive theory does not make a distinction between linguistic knowledge and its use, researchers have also endeavoured to explain the way in which knowledge about the language is stored in the memory and how the process of language acquisition results in automatic comprehension and production of language (O'Malley & Chamot, 1996). The cognitive theory suggests that linguistic codes and structures are stored and retrieved from the memory in exactly the same way as other kinds of information. What is important is the extent to which the learner has acquired formal and functional characteristics of the language and mental processes. This implies the possibility of 'degrees' of knowledge, i.e. the fact that the learner can know something only partially (Ellis, 1995).

The cognitive theory defines L2 acquisition as a complex cognitive skill which, like other such skills, engages cognitive systems (such as perception, memory and information processing) to overcome limitations in human mental capacity which may inhibit performance (Ellis, 2000: 175). The cognitive theory sees memory as functioning in two stages. The first is the *working* (or *short-term*) memory system characterised by limited capacity. This means that short-term memory requires conscious effort and control to retain only modest amounts of information. Short-term memory is believed to be serial in operation. The second stage of storing information is the long-term memory system which is large in capacity, operates in parallel fashion and is not susceptible to conscious control (Atkinson & Schiffrin, 1968, cited in Skehan, 2000). Material is transferred from one system to another by means of phonological and visual repetition in the working memory system, which also contains a central executive component whose task is to direct a limited amount of *attention*.[1] The working memory also holds 'records' from long-term memory that are in the state of 'high activation' (Anderson, 1995) and that interact with new information. The working memory system assumes an important role during intake and speech production. During intake, the working memory has to distinguish what is relevant for comprehension, and in speech production it serves as a 'storage' for storing various elements that are retrieved from long-term memory for the purposes of composing a message. The process of new information acquisition, as O'Malley and Chamot (1996: 17) conclude – citing Weinstein and Mayer (1986) – is a four-stage encoding process involving selection, acquisition, construction and integration. In the first stage, selection, learners focus their interest on specific information which they transfer first into the working memory and then, in the acquisition stage, into the long-term memory for permanent storage. In the third stage, learners actively build internal connections between ideas in the working memory and the long-term memory by making use of related information. In the final stage, integration, learners actively search for prior knowledge in the long-term memory and transfer this knowledge into the active memory.

In sum, in contrast to linguistic L2 acquisition theories, which view linguistic knowledge as unique and separate from other knowledge systems, a cognitive account of L2 acquisition considers language acquisition as being guided by the same principles as other types of learning, although probably more complex in nature (Ellis, 1995).

One advantage to viewing L2 acquisition as a complex cognitive skill, which seems specially interesting for formal foreign language learning contexts, is that it implies a possibility of improving the language learning ability (O'Malley & Chamot, 1996). Because cognitive learning results in general knowledge applicable in a wide range of similar learning situations, this feature of cognitive learning is often underlined as the most significant (cf. Zarevski, 1994).

The cognitive approach has generated research interest: instead of focusing on the learning itself, researchers are now trying to determine how individual learners approach learning. Namely, cognitivists take the view that individuals construct their own reality and, therefore, acquire different types of knowledge in different ways, even in what seem to be highly similar situations (Williams & Burden, 2001). This means that among learners there are *individual differences*[2] in the way each and every one of them acquires the L2. Individual differences are considered a powerful factor in language acquisition. McLaughlin (1987), for example, points out that any attempt at describing the process of SLA must account for the role of individual differences, for it cannot be ignored. A pedagogical implication is that L2 teachers should identify and understand significant individual differences in their learners if they are to conduct effective teaching (Oxford & Ehrman, 1993).

Areas in which individual differences exist encompass a host of variables. These are differently labelled and classified by researchers and include language aptitude, motivation, cognitive style and learning strategies. Ellis (1995) distinguishes three sets of variables. The first one includes beliefs about language learning, affective states (e.g. L2 anxiety, presence or lack of self-confidence) and some general factors (language aptitude, motivation, age, learning style). The second set is comprised of various strategies learners employ in L2 learning, whereas the third set entails language learning outcomes in terms of proficiency, achievement and rate of acquisition. The three sets of variables interact in complex ways, as is illustrated in Figure 2.1 (Ellis, 1995: 473). All variables influence each other, which means that, for example, motivation not only

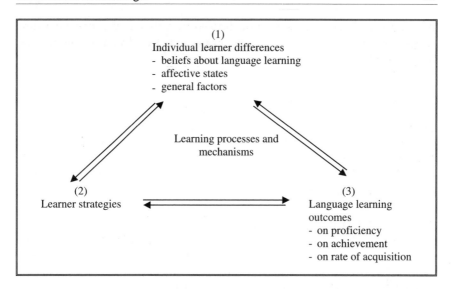

Figure 2.1 A framework for investigating individual learner differences (Ellis, 1995: 473)

affects learning success, but is, at the same time, influenced by it. In addition, the successful use of a learning strategy may result in a higher motivation level or increased language anxiety. In the centre of the triangle there are learning processes and mechanisms which remain hidden most of the time. However, research findings are still inconclusive with regard to the extent to which individual differences affect learning processes.

One of the key notions in the cognitive approach to L2 acquisition is that of *learning strategies*. L2 acquisition is thus defined as a mental process involving the use of strategies that explain how the L2 knowledge system is developed and used in communication (Ellis, 1995). Learning strategies are considered general and related to other types of learning. In the cognitive approach to L2 acquisition, language learners are active participants in the learning process who (consciously) use various mental strategies to organise the language system they are trying to learn (Williams & Burden, 2001).

It is the use of L2 learning strategies that makes the process of L2 acquisition different from that of L1 acquisition.[3] Many theoreticians agree that what the above statement refers to are general strategies for learning an L2 that are not present in the process of L1 acquisition. A slightly different view is advocated by Kaplan (1998), who claims that the L2 acquisition process is characterised by only a few general learning strategies, but that it is mostly governed by domain-specific, i.e. linguistically oriented strategies.

The role of learning strategies in the process of cognitive learning is to make explicit what otherwise may occur without learners' awareness or may occur inefficiently, and thus may result in incomplete storage of information in the long-term memory. Through the use of learning strategies, learners select, acquire, organise and integrate the new knowledge (Weinstein & Mayer, 1986). Learning strategies that activate mental processes are considered more effective in facilitating learning (O'Malley & Chamot, 1996) and they can, after repeated use, become automatic.

Although cognitive theory of learning has received criticism as being one-sided (i.e. neglecting the influence of linguistic factors in L2 acquisition), one could agree, as Ellis (2000) does, that at least two explications may be acceptable: one is an account of how learners obtain control over L2 knowledge (i.e. how learners by interaction or free practising activate strategies for proceduralising knowledge) and the other is an account of how learners restructure their L2 knowledge in order to make it available for use.

The importance of language learning strategies is reflected in the findings of current research which showed that various learning strategies may create different acquisition patterns in individuals acquiring the same L2 (McLaughlin, 1987). Furthermore, many theoreticians and researchers believe that language learning strategies applied by learners in solving language learning tasks[4] are, at least to some extent, responsible for successful language acquisition. The assumption that language learning strategies, as complex cognitive skills, may be taught, implies their significant role in improving general language learning ability.

The following subsections explore in greater detail the role of learning strategies as seen by various applied linguists and their models and theories of L2 acquisition (cf. also Sawyer & Ranta, 2001).

The Role of Language Learning Strategies in Theories and Models of Second Language Acquisition

The quest for a unified and complete theory explicating in an acceptable way the whole complexity of L2 learning and acquisition has been marked by a tendency to create theoretical models in which the factors and variables that play an important part in interpreting L2 acquisition, as well as their interactions, are illustrated.

We turn now to an exploration of those theories and models that recognise individual differences in language learning, that is, to put it more precisely, that view language learning strategies as an important concept in L2 acquisition. It is not our intention to give a comprehensive review of the mentioned theories and models, but to note their relevance for the notion of learning strategies.

Interlanguage theory

Interlanguage theory has brought about the first attempt to describe the process of SLA from a cognitive – and not only a linguistic – perspective. The term *interlanguage*[5] refers to a language system (i.e. grammar) constructed by language learners in the process of L2 learning. Since its appearance in the early 1970s, the term has dominated SLA research for several decades.

The theory views errors made by learners in language production as evidence indicating the development of linguistic competence. What must be accentuated is that errors are not considered to be an extremely negative side effect of learning, but a manifestation of efforts invested by the learner in organising the language input.

The theory explicitly refers to the notion of learning strategies: it distinguishes between (cognitive) learning strategies and communication strategies. Namely, the originator of the theory, Selinker (1972), postulated that interlanguage is the product of five central cognitive processes involved in L2 acquisition: language transfer, transfer of training, strategies of learning an L2, strategies of communication in L2 and overgeneralisation of linguistic material. Language learning strategies appear to be central to this theory according to which interlanguage evolves over time as a result of various strategies that learners use to make sense of the language input and to control the output. Therefore, on the one hand, some elements of the interlanguage may be the result of learners' specific approach to the language material to be learnt, i.e. their selection of learning strategies. On the other hand, use of communication strategies may lead to fossilisation (when learners cease to develop their interlanguage any further), because they enable learners to communicate in an acceptable manner.

Selinker *et al.* (2000) define learning strategies as cognitive activities at the conscious or unconscious level that involve the processing of L2 data in the attempt to express meaning. This primarily refers to grammar learning strategies, i.e. learning strategies that help learners to develop a mental grammar of the L2. It is these strategies that support a definite systematicity in the interlanguage. Errors in production may be caused by the use of strategies such as language transfer, overgeneralisation of L2 rules or simplification. In sum, interlanguage is a single system composed of hypothetical rules that have been developed through different cognitive strategies and are tested and modified by the learner during the process of comprehension and production.

The question that poses itself is why in the original list of five central cognitive processes, language transfer and overgeneralisation are listed separately from learning strategies, although both seem to be examples of learning strategies, and were explored as such even by Selinker and his associates (cf. Ellis, 1995; McLaughlin, 1987), as can be inferred from the discussion above.

Nevertheless, the significance of interlanguage theory lies in the fact that it is the first attempt to take into account the possibility of learner' conscious attempts to control their learning. It was this view that initiated an expansion of research into psychological processes in interlanguage development whose aim was to determine what learners do in order to help facilitate their own learning, i.e. which learning strategies they employ (Griffiths & Parr, 2001). It seems, however, that the research of Selinker's learning strategies, with the exception of transfer, has not been taken up by other researchers.[6]

Bialystok's second language learning model

One of the first theorists who recognised the significant role of learning strategies in the process of L2 acquisition was Bialystok (1978). Her model (also labelled the Analysis-Control Model[7]) is cognitive in nature and is based on the assumption that language is processed by the human mind in the same way as other kinds of information. The model distinguishes, although not always consistently (cf. Ellis, 1995), between processes as obligatory and strategies as optional mental activities (see Figure 2.2; Bialystok, 1978: 71). Learning strategies in the model fall into two groups: formal and functional. Formal strategies refer to accurate linguistic form (formal practising and monitoring), which means that they involve either conscious learning of the L2 or attempts to make the learnt explicit knowledge automatic. Functional strategies refer to language use (functional practising and inferencing), i.e. to learners' endeavours to expose themselves to the target language via communication. Bialystok (1978) states that the

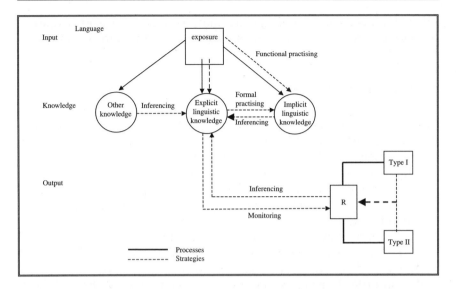

Figure 2.2 Bialystok's (1978: 71) model of second language learning

model includes an additional mechanism that could also qualify as a learning strategy: the possibility to correct a response and return to the Output process line. In other words, it would be a sort of a correction strategy, the concept of which has not been adequately developed in the model.

Strategies are defined as 'optimal methods for exploiting available information to increase the proficiency of L2 learning... They operate by bringing relevant knowledge to the language task that has the effect of improving performance' (Bialystok, 1978: 76). Their use depends on the choice of individual language learners. These strategies connect the three levels of the model (Input, Knowledge and Output). When interacting in the L2, learners use three sources of knowledge (other knowledge, explicit or conscious and implicit or intuitive knowledge), but their choice of learning strategies will depend on the specific knowledge needed for task completion, the difficulty of the task and the proficiency level. Individual learner differences can be attributed to learning strategies used by individual learners (cf. Bialystok, 1979).

The pedagogical implication of this model, as Vandergrift (1995) observes, is the fact that explicit linguistic knowledge can become implicit through a strategy of formal practising. This would suggest that learning strategies can become automatic and, eventually, convert to implicit linguistic knowledge. By the same token, explicit knowledge can be derived from implicit linguistic knowledge through a strategy of inferencing.[8]

Multidimensional Model

The *Multidimensional Model* was advanced by Clahsen *et al.* (cf. 1983). The two dimensions of the model address different areas of development that this model proposes: whereas one dimension deals with acquisitional sequences in interlanguage, the other recognises and provides an explanation for individual learner variation.

In this model, learners are believed to rely initially on non-linguistic processing devices, such as formulas and lexical items that are not assigned to grammar categories, after which they move through a series of stages until they are able to carry out more complex grammatical operations. The relationship between the implicit knowledge and output is determined by indicating learning strategies that learners have to master in order to produce certain linguistic structures. The authors of the model maintain that learners form different paths to the L2. These paths are characterised by developmental stages (defined on the basis of linguistic criteria), but they may vary due to the fact that within stages learners may differ because of their social–psychological orientation, which may range from segregative to integrative. The integrative learner is more likely to achieve higher proficiency levels in an L2, which comes from the use of different learning strategies. A distinction is made between two strategies of simplification: 'restrictive' simplification and 'elaborative' simplification. Restrictive simplification involves omission of elements and morphology. It is characteristic of early learning and learners with a segregative orientation. Elaborative simplification is a learning strategy used by integrative learners in a later stage in the learning process. This strategy involves formulation of hypotheses about second language rules and is seen as a predictor of greater progress in learning.[9]

Adaptive Control of Thought (ACT) Model

Anderson's *Adaptive Control of Thought Model* (ACT) is another model that is cognitive in nature, because it attempts to explain L2 acquisition in terms of a general theory of skill learning (cf. Ellis, 1995; O'Malley & Chamot, 1996; Robinson, 2001). The model is based on the distinction between two types of knowledge, i.e. two types of representations in long-term memory: declarative knowledge and procedural knowledge.

Declarative knowledge refers to knowledge of facts and things that we know, whereas procedural knowledge consists of what we know how to do. The distinction between the two types of knowledge is based on the following three assumptions: (a) whilst declarative knowledge is a concept characterised by 'all or nothing', procedural knowledge can be partial; (b) declarative knowledge is acquired suddenly, by receiving a message, whereas procedural knowledge is acquired gradually, by performing the skill; (c) declarative knowledge, unlike procedural, can be communicated verbally (Ellis, 1995).

The model views L2 acquisition as a three-stage process (cognitive, associative and autonomous stages) during which declarative knowledge (i.e. information stored as facts) becomes proceduralised through practice. The process by which new linguistic knowledge is acquired is different from the process of achieving control over this kind of knowledge. New knowledge is 'declarative', whereas automatic knowledge is 'procedural'. One proceeds from declarative to procedural knowledge by developing control. Many errors in the learner's production can be attributed to the lack of procedural, not declarative knowledge.

As for the role of learning strategies, Anderson's theory provides for two interpretation of the term 'learning strategy'. One is that learning strategies occur in the early cognitive stage when they are conscious, after which they cease to be 'strategic' (cf. O'Malley & Chamot, 1996). The other interpretation suggests that strategies occur in all three developmental stages in the form of 'IF ... THEN' statements. For example, the strategy of inferencing would take the following form (O'Malley & Chamot, 1996: 52):

IF the goal is to comprehend an oral or written text,
and I am able to identify a word's meaning,
THEN I will try to infer the meaning from context.

O'Malley and Chamot hold the view that in this theory, similarly to some other cognitive theories of L2 acquisition discussed so far, learning strategies can be described as complex cognitive skills. They are used consciously in initial stages of learning, but can become proceduralised by practising, i.e. by moving through the cognitive, associative and autonomous stages of learning. However, this difference is not of great significance for research as 'learning strategies can only be effectively studied in the declarative stage, when learners are able to verbalize them', claims Ellis (1995: 533).

Although Anderson (1995) does not distinguish between learning strategies and other cognitive processes, his theoretical analysis of cognition includes a number of cognitive and some metacognitive strategies. For example, a cognitive process that fosters storing information in memory is imagery. Images are also helpful in recalling verbal materials, and relating verbal information to images is helpful in vocabulary learning (e.g. mnemonics such as the Keyword Method or the Loci Method). Another cognitive process that plays a key role in remembering meaningful materials is elaboration. It is also the foundation for development of transfer and deductive strategies that enable guessing from context.

O'Malley and Chamot (1996) call for caution with regard to certain limitations of the application of Anderson's theory to viewing language acquisition as a complex cognitive skill, but at the same time emphasise the advantages of identifying mental processes that can be 'presented' to learners as ways to facilitate learning.

McLaughlin's information processing model

Based on the assumption that a critical period for language development exists, cognitive theory views language development after the critical period as an example of the human-information processing system (cf. Skehan, 2000). This means that, prior to the closure of the critical period, the so-called lateralisation – or the completion of allocation of language functions in the brain – has not yet taken place, so that the human brain is especially sensitive to language input. After the critical period, language development is based on general cognitive modules, meaning that language development can be seen as an example of the human information processing system at work in a way that resembles learning in other domains (Skehan, 2000: 79). Thus, L2 learning is modular but organised on the basis of the three stages of information processing: input, central processing and output. In other words, 'the end of the critical period is the point at which the nature of language learning changes from being an automatically engaged process to one in which it becomes yet another cognitive activity' (Skehan, 2000: 283). Different aspects of L2 acquisition are then supported by cognitive abilities that are best understood if they are linked to the information-processing stages.

One of the most ardent advocates of this approach, McLaughlin (1987), claims that learners' capacity to process information is limited by the nature of the task on the one hand, and their own information-processing ability on the other. Learners can extend this capacity in two ways. The first is *automatisation*, i.e. practising through which activation of skills, initially accessible only through controlled processing, becomes automatic or routinised. Thus, the number of information chunks learners can automatically process increases, which results in quantitative modifications in interlanguage. Another way to extend the information-processing capacity is *restructuring*. It allows for qualitative changes in interlanguage that relate to both the way knowledge is represented in the minds of learners and the learning strategies they use. In his analysis of the relationship between restructuring and learning strategies, McLaughlin (1987) draws on the work of Ellis and Færch and Kasper. The line of argument based on Færch and Kasper's supposition is that internalised rules and memorised chunks of the language constitute learners' declarative knowledge, whereas procedural knowledge consists of knowing how to employ learning strategies and procedures to process L2 information. Ellis (cited in McLaughlin, 1987), on the other hand, categorised the above-mentioned procedures into learning strategies (relating to acquisition of procedural knowledge), and production and communication strategies (relating to language use). Their further classification is shown in Table 2.1 (McLaughlin, 1987: 145). The strategies involved in restructuring are learning strategies. In other words, restructuring can be facilitated by the flexible use of learning strategies. In the early stages of learning, learners often simplify, regularise, overgeneralise and reduce redundancy, which results in creating an internal representational system that is more simple than the input and that relies on L1 and on universal principles of language acquisition. At later stages of L2 development, inferencing and hypothesis testing strategies predominate. 'If learning requires a constant modification of organisational structures, then it is these strategies of inferencing and hypothesis testing that govern the process of restructuring' (McLaughlin, 1987: 147).

In Færch and Kasper's theory learning strategies are considered as part of procedural knowledge. However, the question of how learning strategies become part of that knowledge has still not been satisfactorily answered in their theory (O'Malley & Chamot, 1996).

In sum, L2 acquisition is defined as learning a skill which requires practising until integrated into automated knowledge. Learning is a set of procedures for creating internal representations based on the linguistic system, and involves procedures for selecting appropriate vocabulary, grammatical rules and pragmatic conventions. In line with the cognitive approach, language learning does involve the acquisition of a complex

Table 2.1 A typology of learner strategies (McLaughlin, 1987: 145)

Type of strategy	*Examples*
Learning strategy	Simplification
	Overgeneralisation
	Transfer
	Inferencing
	Intralingual
	Extralingual
	Hypothesis-testing strategies
	Practice
Production strategies	Planning strategies
	Semantic simplification
	Linguistic simplification
	Correcting strategies
Communication strategies	Reduction strategies
	Formal
	Functional
	Achievement strategies
	Compensatory
	Retrieval

cognitive skill, but, at the same time, it involves the acquisition of a complex linguistic skill (McLaughlin, 1987: 150).

Stern's synthesis of models

In his analysis of the state of the art in the field of L2 acquisition, especially the development of theoretical foundations, Stern (1986) highlights the usefulness of the proposed models of L2 acquisition, in that they give a much needed overview of relevant factors and their interactions to be taken into consideration when interpreting L2 acquisition. However, none of the models can be regarded as conclusive and capable of explaining all the phenomena involved in L2 learning. Therefore, he proposed an 'uncontroversial synthesis representing the consensus among different investigators on the main factors that play a role in language learning' (Stern, 1986: 338).

As shown in Figure 2.3 (Stern, 1986: 338), the model (or rather a framework for examination of L2 learning) consists of five sets of variables: (1) social context, (2) learner characteristics, (3) learning conditions, (4) learning process and (5) learning outcomes. The question believed to be crucial is why certain learners are successful while others are not, i.e. what combination of factors contributes to their success or failure.

The fourth set of variables, the learning process (4), consists of overt strategies and techniques used by learners and covert mental operations.[10] In the model, these variables are determined by learner characteristics and learning conditions, and, indirectly, by social context.

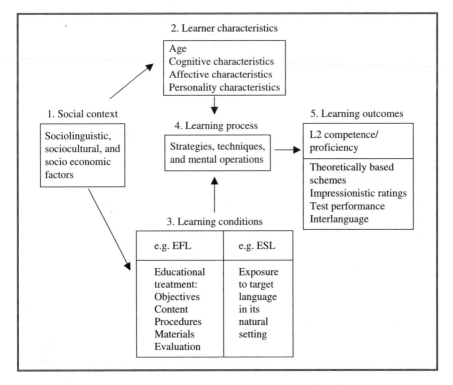

Figure 2.3 Framework for examination of second language learning (Stern, 1986: 338)

They directly influence the learning outcomes. Learners are involved in the learning process in three ways: (1) intellectually/cognitively, (2) socially and (3) affectively. Strategies that (good) learners are likely to employ in this process can be categorised in the following groups (Stern, 1986: 411):

(a) active planning strategy, involving selecting goals, recognising stages and developmental sequences, and active participation in the learning process;

(b) 'academic' (explicit) learning strategies, reflecting learners' readiness to study and practice language rules and relationships; to notice, to analyse, and to develop the necessary techniques of practice and memorisation; to monitor their own performance and revise it in order to make progress towards a higher level of competence in the target language;

(c) social learning strategies, involving a number of strategies such as recognition of initial dependent status, seeking opportunities for communicative contact, and development of communication strategies for overcoming difficulties in communicating in the target language;

(d) affective strategies, which refer to learners' management of emotional and motivational problems, and which include behaviours such as development of positive attitudes towards the self as language learner, towards the L2 culture and society, accumulation of energy needed for overcoming frustrations, and, finally, persisting in their efforts.

All learners do not use the four strategies in the same way for many reasons. It seems safe to assume, however, that failure to learn is caused by an inadequate use of what, in a particular learning situation, might be a crucial learning strategy. Unsuccessful learners are therefore those who do not use strategies adequately, those who are inconsistent in using them or those who have not developed any learning strategies at all. However plausible this explanation appears, it should be treated with caution, i.e. confirmed or modified in light of new evidence from further research.

Abraham and Vann's Model of Second Language Learning

What distinguishes Abraham and Vann's (1987) Model of Second Language Learning is the fact that it resulted from its authors' research into learning strategies. The model was developed on the basis of the

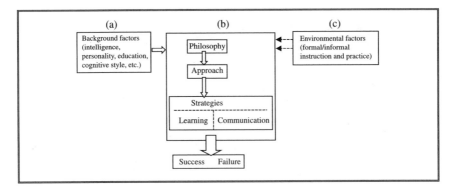

Figure 2.4 Model of Second Language Learning (Abraham & Vann, 1987: 97)

results of an investigation and comparison of strategies used by a successful and an unsuccessful language learner. As can be seen in Figure 2.4 (Abraham & Vann, 1987: 97), the model suggests that learners have a certain philosophy of language learning that determines their approach in language learning situations. This approach is manifested in observable and unobservable strategies used in learning and communication. These factors create a hierarchy and they directly influence learners' achievement, i.e. degrees of success. The model allows for a number of combinations of variables, marked (a) and (c) in the model, that can have both a positive and a negative impact on language learning outcomes.

The authors argue that this model redresses the limitations of previously proposed models by emphasising the significance of background factors and their influence on the learning process. However, they also call for further research in order to test and refine the model.

Ellis's second language acquisition model

In the model of L2 acquisition proposed by Ellis (1995), learning strategies act as a mediator between individual learner differences and situational and social factors on the one hand, and learning outcomes on the other. Those sets of variables determine the learner's choice of learning strategies that affect learning outcomes in terms of level and rate of achievement, but also the other way around: learning outcomes and achieved level of competence may affect the selection of learning strategies. The sets of variables and their interactions are shown in Figure 2.5 (Ellis, 1995: 530).

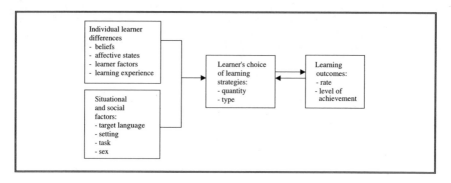

Figure 2.5 The relationship between individual learner differences, situational factors, learning strategies and learning outcomes (Ellis, 1995: 530)

Following Tarone's classification, Ellis distinguishes three groups of strategies: production strategies, communication strategies and learning strategies.[11] The first two groups refer to language use. The learner uses production strategies in the attempt to use his or her linguistic system efficiently and clearly, with a minimum of effort. This group of strategies includes, for example, simplification, rehearsal and discourse planning. Communication strategies help learners to overcome limitations in communication. Learning strategies reflect the learner's attempt to develop linguistic and sociolinguistic competence in L2, the examples being memorisation, initiation of conversation with native speakers and inferencing. Although differences among strategy types are important, the distinction is not easy to maintain, because it is based on the learner's intent to learn or to communicate.

Furthermore, Ellis – again relying on Tarone (1981) – finds the distinction between skill learning strategies and language learning strategies useful. Skill learning strategies refer to the efforts a learner invests in the development of listening, speaking, reading and writing skills.

Cognitive/conative model of learning

Young and Perkins (1995) created the cognitive/conative model, i.e. a general theory of human learning. They assert that their model explicates the diversity of mental representations apparent in L2 acquisition more efficiently then other current SLA theories. Also, they believe, it effectively accounts for individual differences in L2 learning processes.

According to this theory, learning (i.e. knowledge changes) can take place in the following ways:

(1) Vector learning: learners accrete new knowledge (accumulate L2 knowledge) and become more skilful (increase the speed of information processing). In the area of learning strategies, this is manifested by initial limitation, for example, to mnemonics, but acquiring new strategies leads to flexible use of strategies or their adaptation to new tasks.
(2) Interaction of new information with existing knowledge to cause restructuring which may take two forms: the reorganisation of one type of knowledge or the transformation of one type of knowledge into another (cf. the above discussed McLaughlin's model of learning).
(3) Diverse developmental processes due to modularity.

The model recognises five basic types of mental construct: conceptual structures, procedural skills, learning strategies, self-regulatory functions and motivational orientations. Conceptual structures encompass declarative knowledge mostly accessible by conscious introspection. Procedural skills become automatic after practice and trigger fast and skilled performance. Learning strategies are defined as 'specialized ways of processing information that enhance its comprehension, learning or retention' (Young & Perkins, 1995: 150). In the model, strategies are seen as having the capacity to change, which implies the possibility of strategy training, despite the fact that they are deeply rooted in every learner's personal style. Self-regulatory functions provide learners with the ability to consciously regulate their information processing, i.e. with metacognitive awareness, which may influence learning. Motivational orientations refer to motivation for continued learning and achievement, interest in the subject matter, and a sense of confidence and self-efficacy as a learner.

The first two constructs (conceptual structures and procedural skills) are cognitive in nature, for they refer to cognitive information processing. Motivational orientations and self-regulatory functions are conative features of the learner.[12] Both cognition and conation are considered as having equal values in the model. To learning strategies, both cognitive and conative features are attributed: they are cognitive because they affect information processing, and they are conative because they can be influenced by motivation and volition. This indicates that the distinction between cognition and conation is not conceived as a dichotomy, but as one of degrees. Learning strategies include global planning for learning, mnemonics, problem solving heuristics, mapping and structuring tactics using key words detected in reading or listening, and metacognitive processes of comprehension monitoring or hypothesis formation and testing.

The existence of five different types of knowledge points to the modularity of the L2 acquisition process, i.e. the independence of individual constructs. However, interactions among individual constructs are more numerous than can be discerned from the model. For example, learners can modify their learning strategies by conscious attempts to regulate their thoughts and behaviours. In this way, interaction between the two types of knowledge in the cognitive/conative model occurs.

Each cognitive and conative category in the model is characterised by a number of factors typical of the initial state, of the desired end state, or of a developmental transition between initial and final states. Either end of this developmental axis is marked by the so-called distal and proximal construct of aptitude and achievement. Distal aptitude constructs are relatively stable learner characteristics that are difficult to modify, whereas proximal aptitude constructs are relatively malleable and can be influenced by instruction. At the other end of the continuum, proximal achievement constructs (short-term learning goals) and distal achievement constructs (long-term learning outcomes) are placed. With regard to learning strategies, proximal achievement construct would refer to flexible strategy use, and distal goal would be the achievement of a capacity for autonomous learning.

Finally, the model suggests a direction for further research which would, among other things, measure individual differences in developmental processes in all five dimensions or show, for example, how self-regulation affects learning strategies. The significance of the model lies in the fact that it recognises the role of formal instruction which surpasses provision of comprehensible input in Krashen's terms. Future research would, therefore, explore the ways in which teachers, their procedures and teaching materials may influence the development of learning strategies. Furthermore, it is necessary to conduct an empirical investigation into whether there is a difference between 'novice learners' and 'expert learners' in the use of strategies, which would yield information on strategies appropriate for different levels of development.

Skehan's model of individual differences in language learning

Drawing on research on individual differences in L2 learning, Skehan (2000) has proposed an introductory general model incorporating four classes of individual differences: modality preference, foreign language aptitude, learning style and learning strategies (Figure 2.6; Skehan, 2000: 268). Firstly, modality preference concerns the preferred input channel – visual, auditory or kinaesthetic. Secondly, language aptitude entails the ability of phonemic coding, language analytic capacity and memory, suggesting that the learner can have either an analytic or a memory predisposition. Thirdly, learning style refers to cognitive dimensions of holistic versus analytic processing, as well as to visual versus verbal representations. In addition, another learner characteristic belonging to this class is the learner's personality aspect of style which may be either passive or active. Finally, the fourth class of individual differences is made up of learning strategies. The classification of learning strategies into metacognitive, cognitive and socioaffective Skehan adopts from O'Malley and Chamot (see also Chapter 3).

What needs to be emphasised with regard to the model is the left-to-right movement: it implies progressively greater degrees of flexibility; i.e. degrees to which individual differences are amenable to change through instruction. It is assumed that language aptitude and modality preference are rather inflexible features, although learners can learn how to

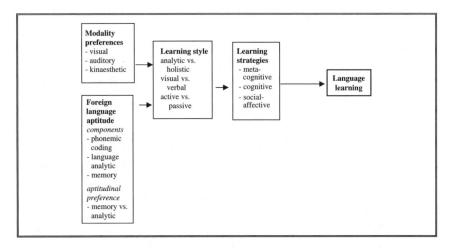

Figure 2.6 Learner differences and language learning (Skehan, 2000: 268)

exploit them to the best degree possible. Changes in learning styles are possible, because every individual commands a range of styles. These changes occur at different points of a style continuum depending on, for example, communicative demands. The model suggests, one concludes, that learning strategies are the most amenable to change of all features, that is that instruction can affect their development and use.

Tentative Conclusion

The L2 theories and models described in this section show both differences and similarities. Some of the differences among the models and theories can be attributed to the fact that their originators laid emphasis on different variables that were, in line with their view, given priority in their research. Another point of dissimilarity between the models is that different labels are applied to important constructs, as well as failure to define these in clear and precise terms. Similarly, researchers ran into difficulties when trying to measure or isolate phenomena they investigated (Stern, 1986).

Nevertheless, all models project assumptions that can, with a few exceptions, be summed up as follows:

- L2 acquisition is similar to learning of other complex cognitive skills;[13]
- the process of L2 acquisition is different from the L1 acquisition: whereas L1 is acquired by means of an inborn language acquisition capacity in a mostly predetermined order, L2 acquisition is governed by the use of learning strategies and is characterised by diverse acquisition patterns;
- learning strategies reflect conscious efforts the learner invests in L2 learning and enable the learner to control the learning process;
- learning strategies affect L2 acquisition process, its success or failure;
- learning strategies are a source of individual learner differences;
- learning strategies interact with other constructs in the models (e.g. conative in Young & Perkins's model, or learner characteristics in Stern's and Abraham & Vann's model);
- learning strategies are the individual learner characteristic that is seen as the most amenable to change: learning strategies can be taught and practised until their use becomes automatic, i.e. until learners become skilled and fast strategy users.

Defining Language Learning Strategies

Having concluded the exploration of several L2 acquisition theories and models, particularly the way they view and interpret the role of learning strategies, we now turn to the concept of learning strategies. The issues to be discussed here are the distinction between learning strategies (hereafter LS) and other related terms, definition of language learning strategies (hereafter LLS), taxonomy and categorisation of LLS, and characteristics of LLS.

What are language learning strategies?

The concept of 'language learning strategy' or 'learner strategy', referring to learners' attempt to learn, has become widely recognised in the field of L2 acquisition, especially after the extensive research conducted by Oxford (*passim*) and Chamot and O'Malley (*passim*). Although the term itself is generally accepted – thus making the other terms[14] redundant – there remain many unresolved issues concerning language learning strategies which are reflected in the following questions.

What are LLS? Do they refer to specific or general behaviour, i.e. what is the nature of 'strategic' behaviour? Are LLS actions, behaviours or functions? Are they behaviours or mental activities? Are they conscious or unconscious? Is their use observable or not? Do LLS affect the development of language competence directly or indirectly? What motivates the use of LLS?

The relationship between LLS and other more or less related terms is viewed in different theories and models as completely distinct, as having common qualities or as overlapping. The above discussion of L2 acquisition models included a few examples illustrating the problem, one of which is the distinction between learning strategies (as learners' general approaches to learning) and techniques (as specific actions) in Stern's model (Stern 1986). Similarly, Goh (1998) makes a distinction between strategies and tactics, with strategies referring to a general approach to learning, and tactics to specific actions. Tactics are observable actions implying the use of a certain strategy (e.g. when a learner infers a word's meaning by remembering another word that sounds similar, he or she is using the strategy of inferencing). Currently, researchers have abandoned the dichotomy between strategies and tactics/techniques and use the term individual LS to refer to the kind of behaviour Stern calls techniques.

Bialystok (1978) emphasises the difference between obligatory, sub-conscious processes, and optional, conscious LS in her model of SLA.

However, in her subsequent discussions, Bialystok allows for the possibility that learners do not have to always be conscious of their strategic choice. She concludes that consciousness as a criterion for distinction between strategic and non-strategic behaviour cannot be applied (Bialystok, 1990). It seems that a majority of researchers agree that the use of LS presupposes a certain degree of consciousness. Cohen (1998), however, asserts that if the strategy is not conscious and the learner cannot control it, it becomes a process.

Some models distinguish between learning strategies, communication strategies and production strategies (cf. Ellis, 1995 following Færch & Kasper, 1983; McLaughlin, 1987; Tarone, 1981). The main criterion for distinguishing between them is the learners' intention. Tarone (1981), for example, views use of learning strategies as motivated by learners' intention to learn, whereas production strategies are motivated by learners' desire to communicate with a minimum of effort. Communication strategies[15] help learners deal with problems in communication. To these, Tarone adds perception strategies which refer to attempts to interpret the received message. These distinctions may seem important, but they are not easily applied when, for example learner's motivation for strategy use is not clear. Even when strategies do have a different purpose, they are not completely independent. A memory strategy is not likely to be used for communicative purposes, but a communication strategy can be used in learning. For example, 'asking for help' can be both a learning strategy and a communication strategy. Moreover, a learner can be motivated to learn and to communicate at the same time, and the possibility of unconscious L2 acquisition during communication cannot be disregarded. The issue of intention is often related to the issue of consciousness, which, as Bialystok (1990) claims, is difficult to investigate empirically. Significant features of communication strategies, in addition to the speaker's intention to communication, include the speaker's belief that one or both communicators lack adequate means of expression and the speaker's choice to abandon the message or employ alternative means of expression (Tarone, 1981). The interaction between intention, belief and choice seems crucial in distinguishing between communication and learning strategies that are not interactive in nature.

It is not clear from the models whether or how communication strategies affect learning. Consequently, some researchers conclude that communication strategies are extremely important in L2 learning because they enable learners to continue communicating, thus creating opportunities for learning through a prolonged exposure to L2 input (Williams & Burden, 2001). In contrast, Selinker (1972) believes that the use of communication strategies can lead to fossilisation as learners cease to learn when they realise that they are able to communicate. Between these two extremes, there is the view of communication strategies as potentially affecting learning (e.g. Cohen, 1998), or as being a type of learning strategy (e.g. Lessard-Clouston, 1997).

Furthermore, some researchers, such as Tarone (1981) and Ellis (1995), find it useful to distinguish between two types of LS: language LS (defined as attempts to develop linguistic and sociolinguistic competence) and skill LS (defined as learners' attempts to become skilled listeners, speakers, readers and writers). Learning strategies are considered superior to skill learning strategies, because they are executive processes responsible for skill management and coordination that are used in attempts to learn an L2. Learning strategies include the ability to monitor the learning situation and respond accordingly. This includes assessing the learning situation, planning, selection of adequate skills, sequencing of skills, skill coordination and evaluation of their effectiveness possibly followed by revision of the plan. Carrell (1989) interprets the distinction between skills and strategies via an active and passive component. Strategies refer to intentional actions selected and controlled by learners in the attempt to achieve a goal, where their active participation is emphasised. Skills, on the other hand, can refer to passive abilities that do not have to be activated. The problem is that the distinction between learning strategies and skill learning strategies is not clear-cut nor is it consistently maintained in the literature on learning strategies. For example, Williams and Burden (2001) use the term 'strategy' to refer to various processes and do not make a distinction between strategies and skills. In their view, strategies are rather to be considered more or less global or task specific, i.e. strategies of a higher or lower order.

Finally, Ellis (1995) and Cohen (1998) advocate the distinction between language learning strategies and language use strategies. Both sets of strategies are defined as actions that learners 'consciously select either to improve the learning of L2, the use of it, or both' (Cohen 1998: 5). Taken together, they constitute L2 learner strategies. Learning strategies include strategies for identifying the learning material, distinguishing it from other (irrelevant) material, grouping it for easier learning, maintaining contact with the material (through classroom tasks or homework assignments, and formally storing the material in memory if not acquired naturally (through the use of, e.g. rote learning, the use of mnemonics, etc.). Languages use strategies, regardless of the level of mastery, consist of four sets of strategies: retrieval strategies, rehearsal strategies, cover strategies and communication strategies. Cover strategies are a special type of compensation strategy because they are used by learners in their attempt to create the impression that they control the material when they, in fact, do not. Communication strategies encompass approaches to conveying an informative and meaningful message. These include intralingual strategies, such as generalising a grammar rule or meaning of a word, and interlingual strategies, such as negative transfer, topic avoidance or abandonment, message reduction, codeswitching or para-phrasing. Although Ellis (1995) warns that language learning is not the same as language use, thus supporting the distinction between language learning and language use strategies, he finds it almost impossible to recognise the distinction in practice. Thus, rehearsal strategies, for example, can be seen as belonging to both groups of strategies. McDonough (1995) asserts that a strict distinction between learning and use would imply that a learner would cease to learn when using the target language in a conversation with a native speaker or when reading newspapers. It is in such situations that an attentive learner learns a great deal. The distinction is, therefore, a matter of emphasis: learning and use can take place simultaneously with language learning strategies and language use strategies overlapping. The issue of this dichotomy calls for further research that would determine whether it has any practical value.

There is still no generally accepted definition of the concept of LLS. Table 2.2 contains a sample of definitions that show a discrepancy in a number of features. These differences are, to some extent, a consequence of the fact that researchers tend to define LS in the context of their own research. Thus, the focus of research becomes the focus of the definition of LLS.

Whereas the focal point of early definitions of LS is the outcome of LLS use, i.e. linguistic or sociolinguistic competence, recent definitions stress processes and characteristics of LLS. Some definitions are very general, while others are quite specific. Oxford's (1990) definition, for example, is very broad as it includes almost every decision made in the process of L2 learning. Some definitions are based on the theory of human information processing (e.g. Chamot, 1987) reflecting an important assumption of cognitive science which sees learning as involving such a process. LLS are special ways of information processing that can make comprehension, learning and storing of information more effective (cf. O'Malley & Chamot, 1996). In this framework, LLS are complex cognitive skills that can be learnt and taught.

Strategies cannot be characterised as inherently either good or bad, but as potentially useful (Cohen, 1998). They are a resource that learners can

Table 2.2 Definitions of language learning strategies

Source	Definition
Tarone (1981)	An attempt to develop linguistic and sociolinguistic competence in the target language.
Rubin (1987)	What learners do to learn and do to regulate their learning.
Chamot (1987)	Techniques, approaches or deliberate actions that students take in order to facilitate learning, recall of both linguistic and content information.
Wenden (1987)	The term refers to language behaviours learners engage in to learn and regulate the learning of L2, to what learners know about the strategies they use (i.e. strategic knowledge), and to what learner know about aspects of L2 learning.
Weinstein and Mayer (1986)	Behaviours and thoughts that a learner engages in during learning that are intended to influence the learner's encoding process.
Oxford (1990)	Behaviours or actions which learners use to make language learning more successful, self-directed and enjoyable.
Ellis (1995)	Generally, a strategy is a mental or behavioural activity related to some specific stage in the process of language acquisition or language use.
Ridley (1997)	Broadly speaking, the term strategy denotes procedures – which are sometimes conscious and sometimes unconscious – used by a person as a way of reaching a goal.
Cohen (1998)	Processes which are consciously selected by learners and which may result in action taken to enhance the learning or use of a L2, through the storage, recall and application of information about that language.
Purpura (1999)	Conscious or unconscious techniques or activities that an individual invokes in language learning, use or testing.

turn to in solving language learning tasks. The element of *choice* seems to be one of the key features of learning strategies. Learners employ strategies intentionally with the aim of making learning more effective. In that way, learners may influence their motivational and affective state, or the way they select, acquire, organise or integrate new knowledge (Weinstein & Mayer, 1986). Learning strategies can have a wide range: their use can influence learning and completion of simple tasks (e.g.

vocabulary learning), as well as of more complex tasks (e.g. comprehension or use of language).

Summarising the definitions quoted in Table 2.2, LLS can be defined as specific actions, behaviours, steps or techniques that learners use (often deliberately) to improve their progress in development of their competence in the target language. Strategies are tools for self-directed participation in learning, necessary for development of communicative competence (Oxford, 1990).

As for the definition of *vocabulary learning strategies*, one may conclude that these are specific strategies utilised in the isolated task of learning vocabulary in the target language. However, they can be employed in all kinds of tasks. For example, Hosenfeld's (1984) list of strategies of successful readers includes a few vocabulary learning strategies, such as guessing a word's meaning from the context, identifying the grammatical category of a word, looking up words or recognising cognates. By the same token, general learning strategies, such as planning or assessment of learning, can be used in vocabulary learning. According to Nation (2001), vocabulary learning strategies are defined by the following important features:

(1) they involve choice;
(2) they are complex, i.e. consisting of several steps;
(3) they require knowledge and benefit from training; and
(4) they increase the efficiency of vocabulary learning and use.

Taxonomy and categorisation of language learning strategies

The existence of the third problem, the lack of an adequate taxonomy and categorisation of LLS, can be attributed to various approaches to defining LLS and to distinguishing between LLS and related terms discussed earlier in this paper, but also to different criteria researchers applied in their classifications. Early classifications, for example, are based on the distinction between LS of successful and unsuccessful learners, whereas some more recent classifications rely on the criterion of direct or indirect effect that learning strategies may have on learning. Oxford (1992/93: 20) sees the existing classifications as falling into the following five categories:

(a) those referring to the behaviours of successful language learners;
(b) those based on psychological functions (cognitive, metacognitive and affective);

(c) those base on linguistic aspects (e.g. monitoring);
(d) those based on language skills or knowledge (e.g. oral production, vocabulary learning); and
(e) those based on different types (or styles) of learners.

However, the categorisation of LLS into cognitive, metacognitive, social and affective seems to be the most widely accepted (*inter alia* Cohen, 1998; O'Malley & Chamot, 1996; Williams & Burden, 2001). Social and affective strategies are often classified into the same set of strategies thus forming the socioaffective group of strategies.

Cognitive strategies concern mental steps or actions that are employed in learning or problem solving, and that require direct analysis, transformation or synthesis (i.e. direct manipulation) of learning material (Rubin, 1987). They include processing language in the human mind and constitute mental processes directly concerned with obtaining, storage, retrieval and use of information in order to learn (Williams & Burden, 2001).

Metacognitive strategies[16] involve planning of learning, setting of goals, thinking about the learning process, monitoring of performance and comprehension, as well as evaluation of results and the learning process. These strategies operate at a different level to cognitive strategies: figuratively speaking, learners look at their learning from the 'outside' (Williams & Burden, 2001). Metacognitive strategies also contain the aspect of learners' awareness of their own strategy use, i.e. conscious control and regulation of adequate strategy use in various learning situations, and enable learners to analyse their own learning. Metacognitive strategies are named in terms of their function and are applicable to various kinds of learning tasks. They are based on knowledge about language learning, i.e. metacognitive knowledge. Wenden (1991) describes three kinds of metacognitive knowledge: person knowledge, task knowledge and strategic knowledge. Person knowledge is general knowledge that learners have about learning or themselves as learners, which includes cognitive and affective factors facilitating or inhibiting learning. Task knowledge refers to what learners need to know about procedures involved in the task in order to complete it successfully. The different aspects of task knowledge include knowledge of the purpose of the task, knowledge of the nature of the task, knowledge of when deliberate learning is required and knowledge of task demands. Strategic knowledge is the knowledge that learners have about strategies, i.e. knowledge about which strategies work best and knowledge about general approaches to language learning that can guide learners' selection of strategies. The role of metacognitive strategies in successful language learning, as Oxford (1990) emphasises, is of great importance, for they help learners not to lose focus of their language learning, and to control their own learning process and progress. In addition, it is important to mention here that the concept of strategic competence, which originally involved only compensatory strategies, has been broadened to include metacognitive strategies. Bachman and Palmer (1996: 70) define strategic competence as 'a set of metacognitive components, or strategies, which can be thought of as higher order executive processes that provide a cognitive management function in language use'. The metacognitive strategy use includes goal setting, assessment and planning, which are not compensatory strategies.

Social strategies entail cooperation with other learners, the teacher or speakers of the L2. These strategies put learners in an environment where practising is possible and they do not affect learning directly (Rubin, 1987).

Affective strategies are learners' attempts to understand and gain control over their feelings (Bimmel, 1993) by using various relaxation techniques, self-encouragement, etc. Although affective strategies do not directly affect learning, their role in language learning is still seen as important. These last two sets of strategies are often taken together and form a category of socioaffective strategies.

Some classifications of learning strategies are specialised. They are based on language learning tasks ranging from isolated (e.g. learning of vocabulary, grammar or pronunciation) to integrative, such as oral communication (Segler *et al.*, 2001). What these classifications are concerned with are the subsets of language learning strategies, which may be seen as being a part of general language learning classifications.

Features of language learning strategies

It is argued that the best approach to defining the concept of LLS is to list their main characteristics. Unfortunately, it is obvious that, similarly to the definition of LLS, these features have not been interpreted in the same way in the literature on LLS. It seems paradoxical that these characteristics are the source of problems in terminology and definition of LLS. Therefore, these characteristics cannot be indiscriminately taken as criteria for distinguishing between strategic and non-strategic behaviours. However, they can contribute to the formulation of a more precise working definition.

(1) LLS are specific actions or techniques used by learners (Wenden, 1987) rather than general approaches to learning as suggested by Stern (1986). According to Cohen (1998) it is best to use the term 'strategy' to refer to all activities undertaken in learning taking into account the continuum from broad categories to more specific strategies.

(2) Some LLS are observable and some are not, for LLS involve both physical and mental activities. Absence of observable behaviour does not imply absence of a mental process (Purpura, 1999).

(3) LLS are problem-oriented, i.e. oriented towards a specific language task.[17] They are efficient and productive in problem-solving (Bialystok, 1990).

(4) LLS contribute to learning both directly and indirectly.

(5) The issue of consciousness and LLS is still controversial. Many researchers agree, however, that LLS are often used deliberately and consciously, but their use can become automatic, i.e. subconscious. It can be concluded that LLS are conscious, potentially conscious or subconscious depending on individual learners and the task they are engaged in.

(6) The use of LLS is motivated by learners' desire to learn, but other factors, such as affective ones, should also be taken into account (Oxford, 1990).

(7) LLS can be changed, i.e. the existing LLS can be adapted, new ones learnt and acquired, and unsuccessful ones abandoned.

(8) LLS are oriented towards the broad goal of development of communicative competence (Oxford, 1990).

(9) LLS enable learners to self-regulate their own learning and become autonomous and effective outside the classroom.

(10) LLS change and expand the role of teachers: they help, facilitate, advise, coordinate, diagnose, cooperate, offer ideas and directions, and participate in communication.

(11) In addition to the cognitive aspect, LLS also involve the metacognitive, social and affective aspects.

(12) The choice of LLS is influenced by a number of factors such as teachers' expectations, learners' proficiency level (Green & Oxford, 1995; Lan & Oxford, 2003), age (Harley, 2000), sex (Dreyer & Oxford, 1996; Ehrman & Oxford, 1989), nationality, learning style, previous experience in learning (Elbaum *et al.*, 1993), education (Ehrman & Oxford, 1989; Peacock & Ho, 2003), motivation, self-efficacy (Wong, 2005), as well as personal beliefs and assumptions about language learning (Bialystok, 1979). Cohen (1998) sees linking learning

strategies to learning styles and other personality-related variables not only as useful, but as necessary. Learner variables, teacher variables and data referring to learning context have to be compared to learning strategies in order to explore their interaction.

(13) LLS are systematic: learners do not incidentally discover a LS; they use them systematically on the basis of their knowledge (Bialystok, 1990).

(14) LLS are finite: it is possible to determine a limited number of LLS, because they are not an idiosyncratic creation of every learner (Bialystok, 1990).

Conclusion

This chapter has provided an overview of LLS and their role in L2 learning as seen by various, predominantly cognitive, theories and models of SLA. Although it is the differences among these theories and models that might be the reason that there are many unclear issues, they all seem to reflect particular common assumptions that make LLS undeniably significant for both L2 learning and teaching. Namely, LLS are central to L2 learning and it is the application of LLS that distinguishes the process of L2 learning from the process of L1 acquisition. For L2 learners, LLS are extremely important as they reflect conscious efforts learners make in learning enabling learners to control their own learning. LLS affect the success or failure in L2 learning. Teachers need to be aware of the fact that LLS cause individual differences among learners. Finally, LLS are the learner characteristic that is (the most) amenable to change: they can be practised until their use becomes automatic, i.e. until learners become skilled and efficient in LLS use. It is the fact that LLS can be taught that makes them most intriguing for both teachers and researchers.

Notes

1. For more on the role of attention see Schmidt (2001).
2. The term *individual differences*, taken from psychology, is widely used in the SLA literature and will be used in this work. However, Gass and Selinker (2001) find the term inappropriate because all factors affecting SLA have to be observed in relation to individuals. They suggest the term *non-language influence* or *factors*.
3. cf. Bley-Vroman's hypothesis of fundamental differences (cited in Lucas, 1998).
4. See Lucas (1998) for an interesting account of a language learning process (based on an analysis of linguistic background and development of the

Polish-born English novelist Conrad) where learning strategies are assigned a major role.

5. The term *interlanguage* (coined by Selinker) is the most widely used term referring to this phenomenon in the SLA literature. The other terms used are *Approximate System* (coined by Nemser, 1971), *Transitional Competence* or *Idiosyncratic Dialect* (Corder, 1967) and *Compromise Replica*, coined by a renowned Croatian linguist, Filipović (1986).

6. For a comprehensive analysis of interlanguage theory see McLaughlin (1987).

7. Analysis and control refer to two basic dimensions of the model. The two dimensions, originally labelled knowledge and control, represent processes.

8. For a comprehensive analysis of the model, see Skehan (2000).

9. A fuller account of the model, including criticism of its linguistic dimension, can be found in Skehan (2000).

10. One notes the resemblance with the framework for investigating individual differences proposed by Ellis (see Figure 2.1). The position of learning strategies is somewhat different: whilst in Ellis's model learning strategies are separated from learning processes and mechanisms, but represent a variable affecting them, Stern sees them as a component of the learning process.

11. See also Table 2.1.

12. These features are more commonly referred to in the literature as affective.

13. Ellis (2000) warns, however, that this fundamental assumption of the cognitive theory is not fully justified.

14. The following terms can be found in the early works to refer to the concept of 'learning strategy': techniques, tactics, potentially conscious plans, consciously employed operations, learning skills, basic skills, functional skills, cognitive abilities, problem-solving procedures, language learning behaviours (Wenden, 1987), thinking skills, thinking frames, reasoning skills, basic reasoning skills and learning-to-learn skills (Oxford, 1990).

15. For more on communication strategies, see Dörnyei and Thurell (1991), Færch and Kasper (1983), Ridley (1997), Tarone (1981).

16. Wenden (1991) labels metacognitive strategies as *self-management strategies*. She lists other terms found in the literature, such as regulatory skills or skills of self-directed learning.

17. For more on the relationship between tasks and LLS, see Oxford *et al.* (2004).

Chapter 3

Survey of Research on Vocabulary Learning Strategies

During the last decades the area of L2 acquisition has been marked by a true explosion of research into language learning strategies that emanated from the first attempt at pinpointing reasons why some learners – under the same conditions – achieve better results than their peers. The studies of good language learners (cf. Naiman *et al.*, 1978; Reiss, 1985; Rubin, 1975; 1987; Stern, 1975) spurred further research encompassing a wide (and still-growing) range of focal points, such as generating a definition and classification of learning strategies (cf. Chamot, 1987; O'Malley, 1987; O'Malley & Chamot, 1996; O'Malley *et al.*, 1985a, 1985b; Oxford, *passim*), the relationship between learning strategies and language competence (cf. Bialystok, 1979; Dreyer & Oxford, 1996; Green & Oxford, 1995; Hsiao & Oxford, 2002; Onwuegbuzie *et al.*, 2000; Politzer & McGroarty, 1985) and the effect of various factors (age, proficiency level, gender, strategy training and many more) on the choice and use of learning strategies (cf. Bialystok, 1979; Dreyer & Oxford, 1996; Ehrman & Oxford, 1989, 1995; Green & Oxford, 1995; LoCastro, 1994, 1995; Merrifield, 1997; Nyikos & Oxford, 1993; Oxford, 1996; Wakamoto, 2000; etc.). The more the body of research grew and new questions and research directions emerged, the more specialised studies were conducted.

Research into vocabulary learning strategies stems from two directions of research. The first one is the aforementioned research of general language learning strategies which showed that many of the learning strategies used by learners are in fact vocabulary learning strategies (e.g. memory strategies in Oxford's classification, 1990) or may be used in vocabulary learning. The second one is the research oriented towards exploring the effectiveness of individual strategy application in vocabulary learning. This early research resulted in the formation of an independent subgroup of learning strategies, namely vocabulary learning strategies. This has led to a more systematic research into vocabulary learning strategies, although still insufficient for drawing any definite conclusions. One of the unsolved issues is a satisfactory typology of vocabulary learning strategies. Lists of vocabulary learning strategies are usually a part of general strategies classifications which show that many multi-purpose strategies may be used in vocabulary learning.

Generally, research conducted so far has revealed that many learners employ learning strategies in vocabulary learning more frequently than in other language learning activities (cf. O'Malley *et al.*, 1885a). When doing so, learners opt more often for mechanical strategies such as *memorisation* (Cohen & Aphek, 1981) or *repetition* (O'Malley *et al.*, 1985a). Such choice of strategies may be connected with the level of knowledge, because beginners, for example, cannot successfully use strategies requiring higher levels of L2 knowledge. On the other hand, some studies confirmed that complex strategies, i.e. those demanding a deeper and more active manipulation of information (such as *making associations*) (cf. Cohen & Aphek, 1980) or the *Keyword Method* (cf. Pressley *et al.*, 1982) result in more successful learning, i.e. longer retention of vocabulary. Such strategies can be used by more proficient learners of the target language. Cohen and Aphek's study (1980), in which participants were asked to describe what aid (i.e. mnemonic) they used in vocabulary learning, showed that different categories of associations (e.g. meaning, sound, context, mental image, personal experience, visualisation of the word, word stress, physical reaction, personal name or symbols) do aid retention, and that using the original mnemonic association is more efficient in retrieval than creating a new one or not using any association at all. This study indicated that strategies responsible for inefficient learning were weak memorisation strategies and underdeveloped strategies of *inductive* and *deductive inferencing*.

The Keyword Method, which is a type of a mnemonic device, has been one of the most popular vocabulary learning strategies among research-ers.[1] Mnemonic devices are techniques based on cognitive processes which are used to enhance retention of material one would otherwise forget. The mnemonics can be classified into verbal (reduction, elaborated coding, semantic elaboration, rhyme and rhythm), visual (imagery, the *Loci Method*, method of spatial page organisation) and mixed mnemonics (the Peg Method, the Keyword Method, association mnemonics, rituals, process mnemonics) (Zarevski, 1994). The Keyword Method entails two steps: learners establish an association between the L2 word with an L1 word that sounds similar (the so-called keyword), and then create an interactive representation that associates the keyword and the L2 word (Atkinson, 1975). In her discussion of the role of memory in language acquisition, Thompson (1987) made an exhaustive survey and analysis of vocabulary memory strategies (mainly mnemonics). Although mnemonics are generally taken as facilitating faster learning and easier retrieval of lexical items, not all of them are equally appropriate to be used in language learning. Their efficiency depends on numerous factors: the time the learner invests in acquiring the mnemonic, the learner's capacity for creating images, proficiency level, learning style, metamemory, cultural elements and situation demanding the retrieval of a given word. In addition to mnemonics, the classification of which differs to some extent from the one proposed by Zarevski (1994), Thomson describes the method of physical reaction, the method of verbal elaboration (grouping of words, connecting words into word chain, and connected words into a meaningful story), as well as other memory-enhancing techniques (self-testing, revision in time intervals, practising in natural situations). Many of these techniques have not been (sufficiently) explored in the context of L2 learning, but one can assume that they can facilitate memorisation of larger amounts of vocabulary and easier and faster recall in a given moment.

The studies of the effectiveness of the Keyword Method predominately indicated its superiority over mechanical rote learning (Atkinson, 1975; Elhelou, 1994; Sagarra & Alba, 2006), when used both by advanced learners, who are believed to have developed strategies (Hogben & Lawson, 1994, 1997; Lawson & Hogben, 1998),[2] and by weaker learners (Avila & Sadoski, 1996; Zhang & Schumm, 2000). Participants in the experiments mainly found the method efficient and fun and were actually using it, whereas learners in control groups opted for mechanical learning or 'unsophisticated' learning strategies (Hogben & Lawson, 1997).

However, this strategy is rarely used (if at all) unless it has been trained. Its efficiency seems questionable, too: although learners using this method may achieve better results, their advantage diminishes with time, which is contrary to its aim, i.e. long-term vocabulary retention (Brown & Perry, 1991). What a number of studies imply is that the Keyword Method is not necessarily more successful than the strategies learners use on their own (Bosiljevac, 1996; Ellis & Beaton, 1995). However, a combination of the Keyword Method with another strategy (e.g. semantic elaboration or inferencing) proved as efficient in aiding the information retention and recall over a period of time (cf. Brown & Perry, 1991; Rodriguez & Sadoski, 2000).

Hulstijn's (2000) view of the role of the Keyword Method in vocabulary learning represents a balance between its supporters and opponents. There is no reason, he maintains, why this method should be 'forbidden' in formal instruction, because it is in line with the principles of vocabulary teaching. It, however, should not be taken as a substitute for other strategies (e.g. inferencing from context), but as their useful supplement. Similarly, its usefulness should not be overrated, because there are cases in which its use is impossible, or is dependent on a number of factors, such as phonological and orthographical similarity between L1 and L2, the word class of the keyword, the possibility of creating a mental image of the keyword, etc. (cf. Ellis & Beaton, 1995).

If asked how they learn vocabulary, the majority of learners would mention the rote learning strategy, which, by rule, entails a list of L2 words and their L1 translation (cf. Lawson & Hogben, 1996). Rote learning seems to be a 'natural' strategy, particularly for beginners who rely on lexical associations in vocabulary learning (Griffin & Harley, 1996). It seems safe to assume that the majority of teachers and researchers would concur that this strategy does not aid (long-term) vocabulary acquisition, that is that learning words in context is far more effective than learning isolated items. However, evidence in support of this view is still in short supply. Qian (1996) set out to find some answers with the use of an experiment involving Chinese learners who are, stereotypically, believed to learn vocabulary by memorising L1–L2 pairs of words.[3] After learning vocabulary in context using the SCANR method,[4] and learning words out of context (using a list of words with their translations), on three occasions learners were given a test in which they had to supply the translation of a given word. The results demonstrated that learning lists of words is more efficient than guessing from context. However, the results were influenced by the process of learning itself that entailed certain advantages for the group learning word lists. Namely, apart from the fact that this is a well known and frequently used learning strategy, this group of learners was given feedback, whereas the learners whose task was to guess words' meanings from the context were working on their own, without an opportunity to check their hypotheses. The fact that the tests required learners to provide a translation also benefited the 'word list' group. The weak test results of the group inferencing from context could probably be attributed to incorrect guessing rather than failure to learn lexical items.

Further evidence in support of the efficiency of memorising word lists was supplied by an empirical study conducted by Prince (1996). In addition, this study showed a high rate of successful guessing from context by advanced learners. Another interesting feature of advanced learners is their capacity to transfer knowledge regardless of the learning strategy used in vocabulary learning. Namely, advanced learners can use a word in an adequate L2 context even if they have learnt it paired with its L1 translation. The strategy of learning off word lists, one concludes, should not be rejected, because it does make certain sense, particularly at beginning stages of learning, but additional strategies need to be introduced which would help learners in creating deeper and manifold links within the mental lexicon.

A popular context for investigating vocabulary learning strategies has been the reading skill. These studies were aimed at determining the strategies of discovering meaning used by learners during reading and their efficiency in terms of text comprehension and vocabulary acquisition. Chin (1999) compared the strategy of guessing from context, the strategy of word formation analysis and the combination of the two strategies used while reading. The efficiency of each strategy, however, depended on the task used in testing. In general, multiple choice tasks produced better results than gap-filling tasks. Word formation analysis requires certain knowledge of suffixes, prefixes and their meanings, whereas gap-filling tasks require a deeper semantic-syntactic knowledge of the word. Learners who inferred from the context or used the combined context/word formation strategy were more successful at such tasks. Although the strategy of word formation analysis, especially if it includes attending to etymology, that is to cognates (cf. Bellomo, 1999), can be very useful, its contribution seems irrelevant if the learner has already successfully inferred the word's meaning from the context.

When reading, learners often use a dictionary to discover a word's meaning or to check their assumptions. An investigation into the use of a bilingual dictionary in reading revealed that, in addition to facilitating comprehension, this strategy affects vocabulary learning and retention (Luppescu & Day, 1995). Indeed, the amount of memorised vocabulary can even be doubled (Fraser, 1999)! Learners find dictionary use strenuous, but useful and necessary (Gonzalez, 1999). However, if they cannot use a dictionary appropriately, if they, for example, look up (too) many words or do not understand the given definitions, learners can become frustrated. This is why learners need to be trained in dictionary use, and need to be provided with opportunities to practise this strategy in the framework of various language tasks.

Contemporary language learning, especially its aspect of vocabulary acquisition, is inevitably linked with the mass media, i.e. television, computers, the Internet etc. In addition to providing a rich and natural language input, the mass media play an important part in learners' lives and should therefore be used for their benefit in language learning, both in and outside the classroom. Watching films, subtitled or not, contributes to incidental vocabulary learning even with beginner learners, especially children (Koolstra & Beentjes, 1999).

With regard to this, one needs to mention the studies of Computer Assisted Vocabulary Learning (CAVL) which revealed that learners can successfully learn words using specialised programmes available on CD-ROMs (Pawling, 1999), using a multimedia system connected to the Internet (Tsou *et al.*, 2002), or even through popular computer games (Palmberg, 1988). The advantage of using computer learning pro-grammes is that learners can control and direct their learning, that is determine the pace of learning and the time devoted to one lexical item, as well as choose materials. Fox (1984) emphasises that computer programmes can be used as sources of information on words that can help learners solve the task and that encourage inferencing from context. This happens according to each learner's inclination: whereas some prefer guessing a word's meaning immediately, others use a wide range of guidelines and instructions before venturing a guess. Computers bring together several dimensions of L2 learning, such as texts, pictures, sound, realistic activities, as well as feedback. However, mere exposure is not a promise of success – it is necessary to integrate different modalities in order to create favourable learning conditions (Kang & Dennis, 1995). In the same way, Koren (1999) warns that learners will not retain over a long time period those lexical items learnt incidentally even from most attractive programmes, unless they invest additional effort into their acquisition.

In connection with CAVL, we need to point out the possibility of computerised exploration of linguistic corpora, i.e. the so-called con-cordancing programmes that enable the learner to look up a word in a variety of contexts. Further research is needed to explore the effect that using such programmes may have on vocabulary learning and acquisi-tion (cf. Cobb, 1997).

Most of the research discussed so far in this section focused on pinpointing the most efficient vocabulary learning strategy. Learners, in fact, use a number of different strategies (cf. Lawson & Hogben, 1996; Sanaoui, 1995). The combinations of strategies and their effect on vocabulary acquisition may be a far more important research topic than the effect of one individual vocabulary learning strategy (Gu & Johnson, 1996).

As in many studies of general learning strategies, researchers set out to determine the differences between successful and less successful learners. According to Ahmed (1989), learners can be categorised on the basis of their strategy use. Successful learners are those who are aware of the learning process, know the importance of learning words in context, and are aware of the semantic relationship between new and previously learnt L2 words. They also use, in addition to dictionaries, other learners as a source of information on vocabulary. Weak learners also make use of a number of strategies, but apply them inadequately (Porte, 1988). Unsuccessful learners generally use fewer learning strategies, do not know how to learn words or how to connect them with the acquired knowledge, and avoid active practice (Ahmed, 1989). Furthermore, they lack awareness of the aspects involved in language learning and have insufficient control over their learning strategies, which is in contradiction of the view that metacognitive understanding of the nature and purpose of the task and a wide repertoire of learning strategies are extremely important in vocabulary learning.

The learners in the study carried out by Graham (1997) seemed to rely on an astonishingly small number of vocabulary learning strategies. They used practically identical strategies, the most prominent one being mechanical rote learning of lists of words and their L1 equivalents. Even more interestingly, the aforementioned strategy was the only single strategy used by unsuccessful learners. However, successful learners reported using a more complex vocabulary learning strategy in listening and reading tasks (e.g. inferring from context, word formation analysis), but both good and weak learners displayed underdeveloped dictionary skills.

As has already been mentioned, strategies of good language learners were explored because it was believed that finding out what they do would help weak learners take over the good strategies and thus improve their own learning outcomes. Still, Porte's research findings (1988) indicate that mere imitation of the good language learner's behaviour does not result in progress. It would be necessary to determine the extent to which failure can be attributed to an inadequate or incomplete use of learning strategies. The author, consequently, suggests that weak learners be aided in their identification of strategies and then, if necessary and feasible, in further development of the existing strategies. Studying learning strategies of unsuccessful learners may provide a valuable insight into the role of learning strategies in vocabulary learning.

In what follows we shall focus on studies of vocabulary learning strategies as a whole, i.e. as a specialised subgroup of general learning strategies. One of the first of such studies was undertaken by Sanaoui (1995). The analysis of diaries of English and French learners, used as a source of information on vocabulary learning strategy use, revealed that adult learners fall into two groups based on similarities and differences in their approach to vocabulary learning. This was determined according to several criteria: the degree of engagement in independent learning, the range of self-initiated activities, ways of recording vocabulary, using those notes and the use of words they learn in out-of-class situations (see Table 3.1; Sanaoui, 1995: 24). Whilst the first group of the so-called 'structured' learners characterises an organised approach to learning, the learners in the second group are 'unstructured', i.e. less systematic in learning vocabulary. This study's intention was to emphasise the importance of directing one's own learning and independence of explicit vocabulary instruction. Keeping a learning diary raised the learners' awareness of their own activities and provided them with a basis for their critical evaluation.

Lessard-Clouston's (1996, 1998) studies in part replicated the ones conducted by Sanaoui, but were limited to specific groups of a few participants. The data on vocabulary learning strategies were collected by means of an adapted questionnaire originally devised by Sanaoui

Table 3.1 Features of a structured and an unstructured approach to vocabulary study (Sanaoui, 1995: 24)

Structured approach	*Unstructured approach*
Opportunities for learning vocabulary	
Self-created	Reliance on course
Independent study	Minimal independent study
Range of self-initiated activities	
Extensive	Restricted
Records of lexical items	
Extensive (tend to be systematic)	Minimal (tend to be ad hoc)
Review of lexical items	
Extensive	Little or no review
Practice of lexical items	
Self-created opportunities in and outside classroom	Reliance on course

with the intention to describe the strategic approach to vocabulary learning and to determine the correlation between vocabulary learning strategies and learning outcomes. As both studies pointed to the limitations of the dichotomous division into structured and unstructured approach to vocabulary learning, a third category, labelled semi-structured approach, was added (Lessard-Clouston, 1996). As no connection between the learners' strategic approach to vocabulary learning and learning success (measured by general result of a TOEFL test and a specialised vocabulary knowledge test) was determined, the author concluded that different approaches can be efficient.

For the purposes of a large-scale study (involving over 700 learners), Stoffer (1995, cited in Kudo, 1999; in Schmitt, 1997; and in Singleton, 1999) designed a questionnaire (Vocabulary Strategy Inventory or *VOLSI*) with 53 individual strategies grouped into the following nine categories:

(1)   strategies involving authentic language use,
(2)   strategies involving creative activities,
(3)   strategies used for self-motivation,
(4)   strategies used to create mental linkages,
(5)   memory strategies,
(6)   visual/auditory strategies,
(7)   strategies involving physical action,
(8)   strategies used to overcome anxiety and
(9)   strategies used to organise words.

The most frequently used was the fourth group of strategies (strategies for creating mental linkages), the domineering one being the strategy of relating an L2 with an L1 word. Stoffer found an interesting piece of information, namely that learners learning a language lexically distant from English (e.g. Russian or Japanese) use vocabulary learning strategies more frequently. Although no detailed data on the statistically supported justification of this strategy categorisation were given, as Kudo (1999) remarks, it is still one of the first attempts at categorisation of vocabulary learning strategies, and therefore worth noting.

The major concern of Gu and Johnson' study (1996), involving Chinese EFL learners, is the comparison of the frequency of vocabulary learning strategy use with learners' beliefs about vocabulary learning, level of development of learners' vocabulary and learning success. The 91 statements of the Vocabulary Learning Questionnaire (VLQ Version 3) devised by Gu and Johnson corresponded to the following groups of strategies: selective attention, self-initiating, guessing strategies (by using the existing knowledge/wider context or by using linguistic cues/immediate context), dictionary use strategies (for comprehension, extended strategies of dictionary use, strategy of looking up words in a dictionary), strategies of recording vocabulary (meaning oriented, usage oriented), strategies of memorisation by repetition (using a list of words, oral repetition, visual repetition), strategies of memorisation by coding (associating/elaborating, creating mental linkages, visual coding, auditory coding, word structure, semantic coding, contextual coding) and finally activation strategies.

As for beliefs about vocabulary learning, although one can acquire vocabulary through context, the results revealed that learners consider vocabulary learning as requiring conscious learning and active use. Mechanical memorisation, as has already been mentioned earlier in this chapter, did not prove as popular among Chinese learners as it is usually assumed.[5] Two metacognitive strategies (self-initiating and selective attention) turned out to be important for successful learning. Cognitive strategies that transpired as the most useful both for general success in language learning and for vocabulary expansion were the following: strategies of guessing from context, using a dictionary for learning, note-taking, attending to word formation, contextual coding and deliberate activation of new words. The strategy of visual repetition turned out to be the least useful. Strategies oriented towards vocabulary retention facilitate vocabulary expansion, rather than general success in language learning. Learners, however, have different approaches to vocabulary learning. Gu and Johnson (1996) uncovered five groups of learners based on their approach ('readers', 'active strategy users', 'non-coders', 'coders' and 'passive strategy users'), which provides evidence to support the view that various approaches can be effective.

The questionnaire as a research tool was also used by Schmitt (1997; Schmitt & Schmitt, 1993) in his studies of vocabulary learning strategies used by English learners in Japan. The results of this research are embedded in his proposal of a typology of vocabulary learning strategy which is currently the most comprehensive typology of (exclusively) this subgroup of learning strategies and therefore needs to be explored in more detail.

In the study, learners of different ages were asked to complete a questionnaire containing a list of strategies, mark which strategies they use or add any other strategy that came to their mind. In addition, learners were asked to evaluate the helpfulness of each strategy, regardless of whether they actually use it or not. The findings revealed that the most frequent strategy was the use of a bilingual dictionary, followed by guessing a word's meaning from textual context. Learners often asked their peers for help and repeated words aloud (probably together with its meaning), studied the spelling and pronunciation of words, and said new words aloud to practice pronunciation. The least popular among Japanese learners was the strategy of comparing English with Japanese words (i.e. checking for L1 cognates), which is not surprising given the fact that the two languages are so different that cognates are virtually nonexistent in Japanese.

The initial list of vocabulary learning strategies was compiled on the basis of relevant literature inspection, learners' retrospective descriptions of their own strategies and teachers' experiences. In the end, the list included 58 strategies which the researchers tried to categorise according to existing classifications of learning strategies from previous research (Oxford, 1990; Stoffer, 1995, cited in Schmitt, 1997). Schmitt extracted vocabulary learning strategies from Oxford's taxonomy of general learning strategies and their categorisation into Social (involving co-operation with others), Cognitive (referring to language manipulation or transformation), Metacognitive (used to control the learning process) and Memory strategies (involving relating the new word with some pre-viously learned knowledge). This classification, however, did not prove adequate for the analysis of vocabulary learning strategies for several reasons. First, some strategies could be classified into more than one group, depending on the different intended purpose of a strategy in different situations. Second, the distinction between Cognitive and Memory strategies seemed difficult to maintain, as, when it comes to vocabulary, both groups of strategies are used in recalling words through some form of language manipulation. In order to clarify the distinction between the two categories, the authors set criteria based on Purpura's (1994, cited in Schmitt, 1997) division of storing and memory strategies, and decided, although not completely satisfied with the solution, to label as Cognitive all the strategies that are not that obviously linked to mental manipulation (repeating and using mechanical means), and as Memory strategies the ones similar to traditional mnemonic techniques (associat-ing, linking with prior knowledge and using imagery). Finally, there is no category in Oxford's taxonomy that would refer to strategies used by learners in discovering a new word's meaning without involving other people. Therefore, the researchers introduced a new category: Determi-nation strategies. The resulting taxonomy of vocabulary learning strate-gies consisted of five basic groups of strategies further divided into Discovery strategies (used for initial discovery of a word's meaning) and Consolidation strategies (used for remembering words)[6] (see Table 3.2; Schmitt, 1997: 207). A pitfall of this taxonomy, as the author himself is

Table 3.2 A taxonomy of vocabulary learning strategy (Schmitt, 1997: 207–208)

	Strategies for the discovery of a new word's meaning
DET	Analyse part of speech
DET	Analyse affixes and roots
DET	Check for L1 cognate
DET	Analyse any available pictures or gestures
DET	Guess from textual context
DET	Bilingual dictionary
DET	Monolingual dictionary
DET	Word lists
DET	Flash cards
SOC	Ask teacher for an L1 translation
SOC	Ask teacher for paraphrase or synonym of new word
SOC	Ask teacher for a sentence including the new word
SOC	Ask classmates for meaning
SOC	Discover new meaning through group work activity
	Strategies for consolidating a word once it has been encountered
SOC	Study and practise meaning in a group
SOC	Teacher checks students' flash cards or word lists for accuracy
SOC	Interact with native speakers
MEM	Study word with a pictorial representation of its meaning
MEM	Image word's meaning
MEM	Connect word to a personal experience
MEM	Associate the word with its coordinates
MEM	Connect the word to its synonyms and antonyms

Table 3.2 (*Continued*)

Strategies for the discovery of a new word's meaning

MEM	Use semantic maps
MEM	Use 'scales' for gradable adjectives
MEM	Peg Method
MEM	Loci Method
MEM	Group words together to study them
MEM	Group words together spatially on a page
MEM	Use new words in sentences
MEM	Group words together within a storyline
MEM	Study the spelling of a word
MEM	Study the sound of a word
MEM	Say new word aloud when studying
MEM	Image word form
MEM	Underline initial letter of the word
MEM	Configuration
MEM	Use Keyword Method
MEM	Affixes and roots (remembering)
MEM	Part of speech (remembering)
MEM	Paraphrase the word's meaning
MEM	Use cognates in study
MEM	Learn the words of an idiom together
MEM	Use physical action when learning a word
MEM	Use semantic feature grids
COG	Verbal repetition
COG	Written repetition
COG	Word lists

Table 3.2 (*Continued*)	
Strategies for the discovery of a new word's meaning	
COG	Flash cards
COG	Take notes in class
COG	Use the vocabulary section in your textbook
COG	Listen to tape of word lists
COG	Put English labels on physical objects
COG	Keep a vocabulary notebook
MET	Use English-language media (songs, movies, newscasts, etc)
MET	Testing oneself with word tests
MET	Use spaced word practice
MET	Skip or pass new word
MET	Continue to study word over time

aware, is that some individual strategies can fit into both the Discovery and the Consolidation strategy groups. Moreover, practically all Discovery strategies can be used as Consolidation strategies.

Schmitt's taxonomy includes only major vocabulary learning strategies based on the author's subjective estimation. It is occasionally difficult to decide whether a procedure qualifies as an individual and independent strategy or is merely one of its variations whose number would be too huge for a classification to be manageable. It is necessary then, through further research, to lay down criteria for strategy delineation (for they are usually used in combinations) and criteria for their categorisation into groups, as well as to agree on their names and definitions.

Schmitt's taxonomy was used as a starting point in designing a questionnaire for research on vocabulary learning strategies conducted by Kudo (1999) in Japan. The aim of the research was to determine the frequency of individual strategy usage and to put together a classification of vocabulary learning strategies. The results confirmed that Japanese learners often use the traditional strategy of mechanical rote learning and rarely opt for the strategies demanding deep cognitive processing, which probably depends on the learners' cognitive maturity. With regard to classification, although the results of the pilot study pointed to the existence of four groups of strategies, the main study revealed only two: direct and indirect learning strategies, which is along the lines of Oxford's classification (1990).[7] Each of the two groups consists of two further subgroups found in the pilot study: direct strategies include cognitive and memory strategies, whilst indirect strategies include metacognitive and social strategies. Interestingly, Kudo (1999) drew the conclusion that strategy use is not necessarily culturally conditioned, which is contrary to the prevailing view among strategy researchers. Although learners often choose to behave in culturally and socially approved ways, 'culture should not be seen as a strait jacket, binding students to a particular set of learning strategies all their lives' (Bedell & Oxford, 1996: 60).

The question whether vocabulary strategy use depends on the learning context was the focus of a study conducted by Kojic-Sabo and Lightbown (1999). Two groups of participants were included: learners of English as an L2 in Canada in one and learners of English as a FL in North Yugoslavia in the other group. The questionnaire used in the study was composed of five sets of questions relating to time, learner independence, vocabulary notes, repetition and dictionary use. The five sets of questions were in fact variables which were used to determine the type of approach to vocabulary learning. The significant difference between the two groups of learners was found in relation to the learner independence variable, which included strategies such as practising and using new vocabulary in out-of-class contexts, and which was preferred by learners of English as an L2. Learners of English as a FL, on the other hand, use the (traditional) strategies of repetition more frequently. Both groups often use the dictionary, which shows the importance of this strategy in vocabulary learning. This study confirmed a correlation between a wide range of vocabulary learning strategies and learning success, the most important factors being learner initiative and independence, and the time the learner spends learning vocabulary outside the classroom. The attempt to determine the different approaches to vocabulary learning brought to light the differences between second and FL learning along with the need for further research on the role of context on vocabulary learning.

The study carried out by Pavičić (1999, 2000) involved primary, secondary and university learners of English as a FL in Croatia. Like some of the above-described studies, this one too had as its goal a proposal of classification of vocabulary learning strategies, in addition to the other two main research questions, the first being how often and what vocabulary learning strategies learners use, and the second being the interrelation between some variables (such as achievement, gender and age) and strategy use. Taking into consideration the limitations of the research method (i.e. a structured, specially designed questionnaire) applied in the study, the author concluded that learners do have a satisfactory vocabulary learning strategy inventory which is influenced by learners' age (i.e. level of learning), implying that more advanced learners use strategies more frequently.

The attempt at classification of vocabulary learning strategies confirmed their complex nature: it was difficult to demarcate individual strategies and decide in which category they fit. The factor analysis resulted in five groups of vocabulary learning strategies: strategies for self-initiated independent learning, formal practising, functional practising, memory strategies and compensation strategies. Each of the groups contributes in its way to vocabulary learning, but it is assumed (though not empirically tested) that a combined use of a variety of strategies is the most efficient (Pavičić, 1999).

Rather than compiling a taxonomy, Hatch and Brown (2000) divide vocabulary learning strategies into five essential steps composed of great number of various strategies:

(1) encountering new words (with sources of new words being reading, watching TV, listening to radio, conversations with native speakers, textbooks, wordlists, dictionaries, etc.);
(2) creating a mental picture (visual, auditory or both) of word form (e.g. relating a new word with L1 words or other FLs with similar sounds, using phonetic script, relating to already acquired English words that sound similarly);
(3) learning the word's meaning (e.g. asking the native speaker for the meaning, creating a mental image of the meaning, guessing from context);
(4) creating a strong linkage between word form and meaning in the memory (regardless of the memory strategy used – as long as it is used); and
(5) using words (in example sentences, collocations, various contexts, conversations, etc.).

All five steps are indispensable in the vocabulary learning process, even if at a minimal level. The extent to which a learner engages in each step is directly dependent on the learning goal. For example, if the goal of learning is passive, i.e. receptive knowledge of certain vocabulary, the fifth step is irrelevant. On the other hand, using words is no guarantee of long-term retention. Hatch and Brown (2000) see the steps as connected 'sieves'. The greatest number of lexical items enter the first sieve (the first step), but only a limited number of them pass through it into the next sieve, or the next step. The process is repeated through all sieves, so that the retained number of lexical item is notably smaller than at the initial input. The greater the number of lexical items that the learner manages to transfer from one sieve to the other, the richer his or her vocabulary is.

Another vocabulary learning strategy taxonomy, illustrated in Table 3.3, was proposed by Nation (2001). Its fundamental feature is that the types of strategies refer to various aspects of vocabulary learning. In other words, this taxonomy separates the elements of vocabulary knowledge from vocabulary sources and learning processes. The strategies of *planning* encompass decisions about which lexical items to attend to, as well as how to focus attention and how often to give attention to the item. Learners need to know which vocabulary they need, where they can find information, which aspect of knowledge is required in a particular

Table 3.3 A taxonomy of kinds of vocabulary learning strategies (Nation, 2001: 218)

General class of strategies	Types of strategies
Planning: choosing what to focus on and when to focus on it	Choosing words
	Choosing the aspects of word knowledge
	Choosing strategies
	Planning repetition
Sources: finding information about words	Analysing the word
	Using context
	Consulting a reference source in L1 or L2
	Using parallels in L1 and L2
Processes: establishing knowledge	Noticing
	Retrieving
	Generating

language task and which strategies may help them in going about these tasks. The strategies for vocabulary memorisation are a part of the third group. They refer to learning conditions, from noticing, over retrieval, to vocabulary generation, which is considered the most efficient learning strategy. Noticing, which includes strategies of recording vocabulary and oral or visual repetition, is the first step leading to a deeper information processing. Further on, strategies of retrieval play a very important role in learning: every recall of a previously learnt word strengthens the link between knowledge and retrieval cue. Retrieval can take several forms – receptive (e.g. the cue is the written form, the information to be retrieved is the meaning) or productive (e.g. the cue is the meaning, to be retrieved is the word form), oral or visual, hidden or open, contextual or decontextualised – and can range over all four language skills. The forms (receptive/productive, oral/visual, hidden/open, contextual/decontextualised) also refer to generation strategies. These include expanding knowledge on already known words by means of word analysis, semantic mapping, using scales, etc. Another example of this type of strategy is generation on the basis of rules via contextualisation, using words in collocations and sentences, the use of mnemonic techniques, and meeting and using a word in new contexts through the four language skills. Each of the three basic strategy groups contains a large number of individual strategies characterised by a different degree of complexity.

To conclude, it is interesting to note that within the field of vocabulary learning strategies new specialised subgroups of strategies have recently been formed. Segler *et al.* (2001) report on studies to be carried out with a view to determining what specific strategies learners use in the framework of using computers in computer assisted language learning (CALL). The authors hope to compile a taxonomy that will primarily be relevant for CALL, but that will help to improve the existing classifications, such as that of Schmitt.

The Issue of Vocabulary Strategy Training

In our discussion of research on vocabulary learning strategies we come to one of the burning questions in the field: that of the prospects of their teaching, i.e. the approaches, advantages and limitations and, most importantly, efficiency of such training.

As findings of the research within the field of vocabulary acquisition and vocabulary learning strategies reveal, strategic teaching is one of the four basic approaches to vocabulary teaching (Coady, 2000), the other three being learning from context (i.e. without explicit instruction);

development plus explicit instruction (stressing explicit teaching at beginning levels and development towards contextualised learning); and teaching through practical classroom activities (with no particular methodological foundations). The advocates of a strategic approach to vocabulary teaching, like Oxford and Scarcella (1994) find explicit strategy instruction crucial in vocabulary learning. It is necessary, they assert, to introduce occasionally decontextualised activities as an addition to extensive exposure to language input, because large amounts of vocabulary cannot be acquired in a short time through language skills only. This observation is especially true for advanced learners. Long-term retention of vocabulary presupposes appropriate strategic support. Besides, by acquiring a repertoire of strategies, learners become independent learners able to expand their own vocabulary and meet their own vocabulary needs.

As there is a growing interest in research on vocabulary learning strategies, it seems realistic to expect that the programmes of vocabulary learning strategy training will improve and develop. Ellis (1995) believes that vocabulary learning is the area where strategic instruction would be particularly beneficial for learners. So far, however, the examples of instruction on vocabulary learning strategies have been sporadic. They primarily relate to experimental research focusing on measuring the efficiency of teaching one (or a few) vocabulary learning strategy on the basis of its application. Some of these studies have already been referred to earlier in this chapter. More or less all studies in question imply that learners possess some form of vocabulary learning strategies inventory, but they do not make a systematic use of it, and therefore are in need of instruction. For example, learners know surprisingly little about the use of mnemonics that can help them to integrate new material in the existing cognitive units or to retrieve the acquired via specific cues (Thompson, 1987). One of the reasons could be the fact that vocabulary learning is more often than not left to the learners. Graham (1997) has concluded, on the basis of research involving advanced FL learners in Great Britain, that teachers should primarily encourage learners to experiment with a variety of strategies in order to overcome the domineering strategy of mechanical rote learning of word lists. Furthermore, from the work of Oxford and Rubin, Graham selects the following strategies that need to be instructed:

(1) writing words on word cards, with their meaning on the back;
(2) systematic grouping of words (e.g. according to topic, function, etc.);
(3) saying words out loud while learning;

(4) recording words on tape and listening to it;
(5) connecting words with pictures or to similarly sounding words in L1;
(6) connecting words with situations;
(7) connecting words with places (e.g. its position in the notebook);
(8) the Keyword Method;
(9) natural associations (e.g. antonyms);
(10) learning related words (e.g. according to their suffix).

Although there seems to be an agreement among theoreticians on the need for strategy instruction, few programmes and models of training vocabulary learning strategies have been proposed. Teaching this subgroup of learning strategies has, admittedly, been a component of some programmes for training general learning strategies.[8] An advantage to integrating vocabulary learning strategy training into general training programmes is that many general strategies (such as metacognitive or affective) should be used in vocabulary learning, too. As vocabulary learning strategies are in fact a subgroup of learning strategies, any general guidelines and principles of strategy training may, plausibly, serve as a basis for the development of a comprehensive training programme of vocabulary learning strategies. Such a programme would – in addition to sharing the problems with general strategy training programmes – have its own specific issues to consider. Planning a strategy training programme involves four steps, says Nation (2001): decision on the content, decision on time devoted to strategic teaching, developing a teaching plan for every strategy, and monitoring and giving feedback to learners on their strategy use.

The first step, deciding on the content, refers to the question of which vocabulary learning strategies should be taught. Thompson (1987) points out that research on efficiency of individual strategies is more than necessary, because objective criteria for selection of those most helpful in vocabulary learning can be determined only on the basis of their findings. Nation (2001) sees the usefulness of strategic training in the fact that most of vocabulary learning strategies can be applied in learning various lexical units (e.g. collocations) and in all learning stages.

As for the second step, it is difficult to determine the optimal time one should devote to strategic training, but a mere demonstration or explanation of a strategy is without doubt insufficient. If one takes into consideration that learners need to first understand the goal of strategy use, know in which conditions each of them is efficient, have the knowledge necessary to apply the strategy and, finally, practise their use in various tasks and activities, it becomes clear that meeting the aforesaid goals is time-consuming. However, as Nation (2001) stresses, both learners and teachers can, in the long run, profit from the time invested.

The plan for strategic teaching has to involve all aspects of knowledge and predict an adequate amount of activities and tasks for learners to develop gradually into independent strategy users. Teachers have several patterns of strategic teaching at their disposal, the order of which they can determine to suit their learners' needs:

- The teacher demonstrates the use of the strategy.
- Steps involved in the strategy are separately practised.
- Learners in pairs use the strategy, supporting each other.
- Learners report on their strategy use.
- Learners report on the difficulties and success in strategy use outside the classroom.
- Teachers systematically test the use of strategy and provide feedback.
- If needed, learners consult the teacher on their strategy use.

A plan like this (or a 'mini plan') needs to be designed for every single vocabulary learning strategy, especially if it is a complex one (i.e. consisting of several steps) whose use requires specific knowledge and skills. Also, learners rarely spontaneously use some of the complex strategies (the Keyword Method) unless they have been explicitly trained. Teaching such strategies, therefore, needs to be planned with great care. Nation (2001) has developed an approach to teaching the strategy of guessing from context and the use of word cards, Schmitt and Schmitt (1995) has proposed a plan for teaching the strategy of recording vocabulary, whilst Hulstijn (2000) has offered the guidelines for teaching the Keyword Method which partially touch upon other vocabulary learning strategies. We shall return to these 'mini plans' later in this chapter.

As with general learning strategies, a precondition for successful training of vocabulary learning strategies is the extent to which the teacher is informed. Teachers need to know which vocabulary learning strategies exist and what form of knowledge and skills learners need to acquire in order to successfully use each of them. The authors of the course for educating teachers for Strategy-Based Instruction, Weaver and Cohen (1997) devote one of their course units to training vocabulary learning strategies. The unit has the following structure:

(1) Immediate experience in vocabulary learning. Participants are given the task of learning word lists and are instructed to pay attention to the ways in which they learn them, i.e. to learning strategies. After the task is completed, they are given a short test to check the acquisition level.

(2) Discussion in small groups on efficiency in vocabulary learning, including a description of strategies used by participants.

(3) Accumulation of all vocabulary learning strategies mentioned by the participants.

(4) The course leader extends the list by adding new strategies and gives explanations. This is followed by a discussion on the possibilities of strategy transfer to new tasks.

However, we believe that one lesson is insufficient for training vocabulary learning strategies. Although some vocabulary learning strategies seem easy to teach by giving straightforward advice (e.g. 'Say the words out loud when you learn them, because you will remember them better!'), the descriptions of teaching procedures that follow will show that many strategies are complex in nature, which makes teaching a long-term and demanding mission.

The Keyword Method, as has already been established, requires special training if it is to be used by learners. Hulstijn (2000) suggests leading an initial discussion on individual experiences in vocabulary learning with the teacher encouraging consideration of various mnemonic techniques. The discussion is not to be limited on one mnemonic, because a multiple elaboration is more effective (cf. Hogben & Lawson, 1994). Learners tend to list such strategies as relating the words to their cognates, word formation analysis, sound associations (e.g. rhyming words), non-verbal association (e.g. feeling of pleasure), etc. The teacher then gives a few examples of usage of the Keyword Method, after which learners have a go at practising on a few examples of, first, concrete and then abstract words. The goal is to raise learners' awareness on the criteria for keyword selection (sound similarity and a semantic feature to create a linkage to the target word meaning), and on the values and limitations of the method. For the strategic training to be successful, learners need to have ample opportunities to apply the Keyword Method in real vocabulary learning situations and to share their experiences. It is also important to include the vocabulary learnt by means of this strategy in vocabulary tests because it provides the learners with an opportunity to apply the strategy successfully.

Long-term L2 lesson planning should include a regular introduction of activities fostering the usage of the Keyword Method. Learners should occasionally be tested on the words to be learnt which often reveals a few 'difficult' words. The Keyword Method is especially suitable for such cases. The teacher and learners can jointly create associations, which can be even stronger and more effective than working individually, although it seems right to let learners select their own keyword. It is recommended that learners be encouraged in noting the keyword and other necessary information in their vocabulary notebooks.

The Keyword Method, of course, does not guarantee a long-term vocabulary retention. It is necessary, therefore, to consciously and deliberately revise words and their relevant features (orthography, meaning, grammar and syntactic features, etc.) periodically. Every revision should include retrieval of as many associations created while learning as possible, because such elaborated revision has proved more effective than mechanical.

We move now to the teaching of another complex strategy: guessing or inferring from context. Its usefulness is manifold: in addition to being applicable in various language skills and tasks (reading, listening, learning of low-frequency words), it is one of the crucial strategies in the framework of incidental implicit vocabulary learning. As it is an extremely complex strategy consisting of several steps (such as determining the word class, immediate context analysis, broad context analysis, word formation analysis, substitution), whose successfulness is dependent on several factors (a variety of skills and knowledge), teachers should assist their learners to develop into its skilful users. Nation's (2001) description of the teaching procedure suggests that one needs to focus on the following:

(a) Text and word selection. At least 95% of the words in the text should be familiar to the learners in order for them to be able to use the guessing 'keys'. The selected words need to be inferable from context.
(b) Time. The teaching needs to take place over a long period of time and at frequent intervals. Learners need to have sufficient practice in order to guess quickly without deliberately having to go through all the steps involved in the strategy.
(c) Gradualness and comprehensiveness. Learners need to go through all the steps, working in groups, in pairs or individually, with the pace increasing gradually. The teaching can follow the procedure

according to the above-mentioned possibilities of creating a 'mini plan'.
(d) Activities. Teachers need to know how to analyse critically and select activities to improve the use of this strategy.

The word card strategy is often used in L2 vocabulary learning, but probably with differing success and degree of systematicity. The efficiency of vocabulary learning by means of word cards depends on the way they are used. Like the other complex strategies, this one consists of a few steps which reveal the connection with some other strategies, such as mnemonic techniques, metacognitive strategies of planning or cognitive strategies of revision. The following are the steps in question:

(a) The choice of the lexical item. Learners need to learn and note useful, i.e. frequent lexical items, and avoid confusable ones.
(b) Creating word cards. Cards need to be of smaller size (5 × 4 cm). The word to be learnt (separately or in a sentence) is written on one side of the card, and its meaning (preferably its L1 translation to which a picture can be added) is written on the other. Although other information can be included (collocations, grammar features, etc.), word cards should be kept as simple as possible. The number of lexical items depends on their difficulty: the more difficult the words, the fewer word cards should be made.
(c) Using word cards. The word cards are used in recalling the word's meaning or its form (written on opposite sides of the card), by which a strong connection in the memory is established. One first has to learn receptively (recalling the meaning) and then productively (recalling the form). The order of word cards needs to be changed in order to avoid the effect of 'serial learning' where one word stimulates the recall of the next one. The more difficult words should be placed at the beginning. When revising, it is useful to say the words aloud and to try to use them in a collocation or sentence. It is necessary to put extra effort into remembering the word: here, mnemonic devices can be of use.

It is the teacher's task to make learners aware of the benefits of the steps listed above and of what each of them includes. Also, learners need to be assisted in the usage of this strategy and provided with opportunities to share their learning experiences. Finally, teachers and learners should cooperatively monitor and evaluate the efficiency of using this strategy, discuss the advantages and limitations, and possibilities of its improvement.

One of the vocabulary learning strategies often neglected by teachers is keeping vocabulary notebooks. Following the principles of memory and findings of SLA research, Schmitt and Schmitt (1995) have designed a practical guide for teachers for introducing this strategy in their teaching. The strategy of keeping a well organised vocabulary notebook is time-consuming and strenuous, and learners need to be constantly encouraged not to give up and to understand its advantages. The teacher's task is to gradually lead his or her learners in expanding their knowledge of words, simultaneously providing them with information on new vocabulary learning strategies and with opportunities for revising previously learnt words. In the example given by the authors, a procedure lasting for a few weeks is described. In the first step the teacher explains the aim and the purpose of keeping a vocabulary notebook as an important and obligatory part of L2 learning. It is recommended – for reasons of practicality – that loose-leaf notebooks or word cards be used. After the teacher has presented about 10 words, learners – using the dictionary information – write the translation or synonym on the first page and the new word on the back of the same page. Learners also independently choose another 10 words they wish to learn. Every following day of the week new information on words is added that learners mostly find in dictionaries, but with the teacher's guidance. For example, on the third day the phonetic transcription and the word class are added, and on the fourth learners write the definition in L2. Learners can note additional information they find useful (e.g. illustration of meaning, illustration of the keyword, collocation, semantic clusters, an example sentence, etc.). The teacher should check the notebooks, or even mark them, especially if learners find it motivating. On weekends, learners should study the words, ordering them according to the degree of knowledge. Although not suggested by the authors, the procedure could be extended here to teaching memory strategies through, for example, discussing possible ways of learning vocabulary. The week after, new words are introduced in the same way, but information on each word's derivatives is added. Each week a new strategy can be introduced. The authors favour explicit teaching on strategy use, but do not give any instructions or recommendations for a procedure. With time, learners go through the steps faster and would only need an occasional reminder. The teacher has to check the notebooks regularly for the correctness of the information noted, but also to gain an insight into the level of vocabulary acquisition (grouped by the learners on the basis of their subjective estimate) and into the usage of vocabulary learning strategies. The authors believe that keeping this type of notebook is much more interesting than the traditional note-taking: the former makes learners active participants in the learning process long enough to achieve noticeable results.

None of the vocabulary learning strategies discussed in this section is favoured by the researchers as superior. Quite the opposite: their view is that it is a combination of various strategies that is the most efficient and useful, as they complement each other. For this reason teaching vocabulary learning strategies has to be as comprehensive and balanced as possible, i.e. adapted to the learners' needs in a concrete learning situation.

Vocabulary Learning Strategy Research Methods

One of the issues that researchers of L2 (vocabulary) learning strategies have faced is finding suitable and effective procedures, methods and instruments for identification and classification of strategies. Certain periods in the research on learning strategies were marked by the preference for a certain research method. In terms of methods, research on vocabulary learning strategies has, naturally, followed the same course of development, either as part of general learning strategies or as their specialised subgroup.

The list of available methods initially included classroom observation, analysis of video and audio recordings, verbal learner and teacher reports and guided learning diaries only to be extended by interviews, questionnaires, retrospective self-observation and, finally, the use of computers in learning strategy evaluation. McDonough (1995) makes a distinction between indirect and direct methods. In indirect methods (e.g. questionnaire, discourse analysis), learners decide on the degree of their agreement with a statement drawn up by the researcher, whereas direct methods (e.g. diary, interview) require learners to report on what they do when carrying out a language task. No method prevails in current research: every method has its supporters and opponents, just as every method has its pros and cons. This section focuses on an analysis of the important research methods and instruments, i.e. their advantages and disadvantages, and explores the possibilities of their triangulation.

Researchers can gather data on learning strategies through *observation* (and recording) or through videotaping learners and their behaviour in a concrete classroom situation. The very first research in which this method was used indicated a number of drawbacks (cf. Cohen, 1987; Rubin, 1975). The key problem is that many strategies are mental processes whose use is not manifested in observable behaviour. This means that observation will reveal only those strategies whose application is visible, such as note-taking, asking questions, etc. If a researcher wants to explore such strategies, then observation is a suitable method (Cohen & Scott, 1998) whose main advantage is a high degree of objectivity. Another problem is the initial labelling of the strategies on which coding of the observed behaviour – and consequently the interpretation of the data – will be based. If a structured observation form is used, this method can be used to gather quantitative data suitable for statistical analyses. Such an observation form was used by O'Malley and his colleagues in their 1983 research, but observation did not turn out to be a successful research method in this study (O'Malley & Chamot, 1996).

An additional point needs to be considered with regard to observation, namely the role of the observer. There are a few pitfalls to be aware of: the danger of subjective interpretation of strategic behaviour (e.g. due to expectations created in advance), the inability to observe all learners and all events in the classroom, or paying excessive attention to 'obtrusive' learners. One way of dealing with these problems could be involving a greater number of observers or using additional research methods to complement the data. The fear that the presence of a 'foreign' person or video camera can influence the usual learner behaviour is to an extent well founded, but the problem of learners' changing their behaviour diminishes as the number of observations rises (Cohen & Scott, 1998).

Verbal reports require learners to verbally relate to what they believe they are doing while working on a language task (McDonough, 1995). They are considered a useful and rich source of information on the basis of which one can hypothesise about mental processes, but still are not acceptable as evidence that confirm those hypotheses. The method involves a host of procedures (or their combination) for gathering data before, during and after task completion, such as self-reports (generalised statements about one's own actions), self-observation (introspective or retrospective noticing of specific actions) and self-discovery (or the so called 'think-aloud' procedure, i.e. following the stream of consciousness while performing a task). The directness of the method provides an insight into what information the learner attends to during task completion.

As one of the disadvantages of this method McDonough (1995) stresses the fact that the data are not easily interpretable and generalisable, and that one cannot get information on what it is the learner *does not* attend to. Besides, many cognitive processes are unconscious and therefore inaccessible, or are too complex to be verbalised, which means that participants are required to have a certain level of verbal faculties. Cohen and Scott (1998) warn that participants may feel pressurised to produce verbal responses that are not related to their real cognitive processes and to give 'socially acceptable' statements. Wenden (1991), who already in her early works warned of the inevitable subjectivity of the method, suggests introducing more concrete and specific instructions in order to make the method more structured, as well as complementing it with other research methods. One should not neglect the danger of reactive influence of the verbalisation process on task performance, although Ericson (1988) claims that verbalisation may slow down, but does not alter the process of task completion. The results may, however, depend to a large degree on the participant (i.e. his or her eloquence or word choice in describing the actions, the proficiency in the language in which he or she reports), on the materials used, instructions given, etc. Anderson and Vandergrift (1996) suggest four precautionary measures to be taken as a safeguard against the inefficiency of the method: (a) learner training; (b) collecting data during or immediately after learners' completing the task; (c) in case of retrospective reports, reminding learners of the context of similar task completion (by using, for example, a video recording of the participant); and (d) freedom of choice of the language in which the learner is to report.

Information on learners' strategy use over a longer period of time can be collected by means of learner *diaries*. A special kind of diary is the so called 'dialogic diary', which, in addition to notes made by the learner, contains long responses or short comments of the 'reader' (researcher, teacher or other learners). The method is, in a way, a subtype of verbal reports, because diaries are often retrospective, i.e. written after a task completion. With regard to diaries, two more serious disadvantages can be added to the drawbacks discussed in relation to verbal reports: diversity of data (because the topics are usually selected by the learner) and quantity of data which may only in some segments refer to learning strategies and are therefore not adequate for hypotheses testing and making generalisations (Cohen & Scott, 1998; O'Malley & Chamot, 1996). On the other hand, diaries are suitable for collecting qualitative data on specific strategies used by individual learners. Learner diaries were also used in Halbach's (2000) study, which revealed great differences between successful learners, who described many learning strategies, and unsuccessful learners, who were not able to evaluate their own actions. In a study carried out by Oxford *et al.* (1996) learners were instructed to write about their listening strategies, as well as their grammar and vocabulary learning strategies. The researchers were able to extract quantitative data on the basis of which they explored the differences between male and female participants. Still, as the most useful result of using a verbal report method, these, like many other researchers (cf. Matsumoto, 1996), emphasise the fact that keeping a diary is a metacognitive activity which facilitates learners' awareness raising, but which also provides teachers with useful information on his or her learners' learning habits.

Learners' attempts at remembering past experiences in language learning result in the so-called *learner histories*. An obvious problem is the inability to remember exactly or a distortion of certain experiences or important details due to a large time gap of what may be between a few months to several years. However, it is the time gap that can make such reports more objective than immediate reports. Learner histories may represent a summarised, yet comprehensive picture of a language learning experience. Such reports can have many forms: a written story or a story told and recorded during an interview. In the above-mentioned research by Oxford *et al.* (1996) the participants even used the form of a poem! As this method presupposes a high degree of poetic freedom, the data collected may be rather unstructured. For all these reasons, learner histories are to be considered individualistic, and possibly distorted learning anecdotes (Cohen & Scott, 1998).

The next method we turn to in our analysis are *interviews*. They contain sets of questions whose form, wording and order are determined by the researcher in advance. An example of this is the so-called *General Interview Guide* used by O'Malley *et al.* (cf. O'Malley & Chamot, 1996) in their studies. Interviews can be more or less structured, thus giving the interviewee more or less freedom in selecting the information to be given in response. The researcher does not have complete control over responses, but has the possibility of asking additional questions or clarifications and of asking questions that were not originally predicted. The answers can be extremely diverse, which makes the interpretation of the results difficult. Interviews can be conducted with one participant or with a group simultaneously. With group interviews, there is the danger of mutual influence of the participants (O'Malley & Chamot, 1996), talkativeness of an individual and of the influence of the researcher who is responsible for the atmosphere during interviews. Group interview can turn into a discussion, which gives the retrospection a 'public' dimension that may give participants an insight into other people's way of learning (Matsumoto, 1996). Responses given during interviews may depend on the participant's evaluation of his or her own actions and mental processes, i.e. of the degree of their awareness of learning. As a possible way of surmounting this problem, Cohen and Scott (1998) suggest that learners be instructed to concentrate on recent strategy use or on specific language task or situation, or that the interview be carried out immediately after task completion.

Similar to interviews, *questionnaires* require participants to give answers to a set of (close or open-ended) questions prepared in advance, but – unlike during interviews – the researcher cannot intervene. The main feature of a high-quality questionnaire is a high degree of structure with regard to content, wording and order of questions, which entails a high degree of control exercised by the researcher. When compiling a questionnaire, the researcher must word the questions carefully: for example, ambiguities or suggesting a desirable answer must be avoided. Uniformity of data obtained by means of questionnaire has two major advantages: first, the data lend themselves to statistical analyses, i.e. exploration of mutual correlations or correlations with other variables, and second, the results can be generalised. The most famous structured questionnaire is Oxford's *Strategy Inventory for Language Learning* (SILL) (1990), which has been used in a number of studies worldwide in its original, adapted or translated version (cf. Ančić, 2003; Bremner, 1999; Dreyer & Oxford, 1996; Hsiao & Oxford, 2002; Kaylani, 1996; Mihaljević Djigunović, 1999, 2000; Purpura, 1999; Wakamoto, 2000; Wharton, 2000). The questionnaire is also a popular method in researching vocabulary learning strategies (inter alia Gu & Johnson, 1996; Pavičić, 1999; this volume; Sanaoui, 1995; Schmitt, 1997). Data gathered by means of questionnaires reveal what learners think or believe they do and not what they *really* do (McDonough, 1995) and should be interpreted accordingly. A comparative advantage of questionnaires is the possibility of collecting data from a large number of participants in a relatively short time. It also makes possible the use of statistical procedures in data analysis, i.e. hypothesis testing. As questionnaires are usually anonymous it is assumed that participants are relaxed and honest.

The current technological progress has inevitably resulted in attempts at using computers in monitoring and noting the use of learning strategies (cf. Baily, 1996; Liou, 2000). What is meant by this is a variety of computer programmes installed alongside language learning programmes involving different language tasks (e.g. writing, reading, multiple choice tasks, gap filling, grammar exercises, etc.). An advantage of this method is that monitoring can take place with or without learners' awareness and without interfering with the task completion. The data collected in such a manner would be objective, because they are not based on learners' reports of any kind. The programmes are designed to monitor the use of specific strategies, such as the use of installed resource materials (dictionaries, grammar books, guides for task completion), speed of reading or writing, the order of working on parts of text, etc. As much as this may sound appealing, it can be a limiting feature of this method: all the strategies not resulting in concrete use of the computer programme would remain unnoticed and unmarked. This makes listening or speaking strategies practically impossible to monitor via these programmes. One should note the usual problems connected with the use of technology, such as costs, lack of adequate software, lack of computer skills, etc. (Cohen & Scott, 1998).

Selinker *et al.* (2000) have proposed another additional approach to strategy research: a *workshop*. Generally, they find the method ideal for collecting data on events that are difficult to explore. As the use of learning strategies depends on a host of different factors (individual characteristics, type of the task, etc.), a workshop can be a valuable source of information on them. A workshop combines different research methods (e.g. think aloud, retrospective reports) with the primary goal being determining ways of discovering learning strategies used or believed to be used by an individual. A workshop usually begins by demonstrating an example of a conversation between a researcher and a participant who jointly try to discover the participant's learning strategies. A demonstration is followed by a discussion involving all workshop participants on the basis of which conclusions are drawn.

Conclusion

In this chapter, the discussion of vocabulary learning strategies followed three threads: first, studies of vocabulary learning strategies were critically reviewed, next, the issue of vocabulary learning strategy training was considered, and, lastly, methods and instruments of vocabulary learning strategy investigation were mapped out.

As for the research methods, a final remark needs to be made: as has been indicated earlier in this chapter, the answer to the question of which method to choose lies not in the discovery of one 'perfect' method, but in a combination of those that complement each other in the best way. The type, number and details of learning strategies reported by participants will depend on the method used, as O'Malley and Chamot (1996) conclude. Therefore, researchers agree – many on the basis of their own direct comparison of methods (cf. Levine & Reves, 1998) – that it is necessary to use a combination of qualitative and quantitative data, the so-called triangulation, which would render reliable conclusions on language learning strategies and their use (cf. Cohen, 1998; Cohen & Scott, 1998; McDonough, 1995; O'Malley & Chamot, 1996). Triangulation has already been used in many studies (cf. Lawson & Hogben, 1996; Naiman *et al.*, 1978; O'Malley & Chamot, 1996). The selection of the method (or methods) will, however, depend on a number of factors, some of which are the following:

- purpose and aim of research (e.g. hypothesis testing or determining specific strategies used by an individual learner);
- the type of strategies being explored (e.g. only metacognitive);
- language skill or knowledge (listening, vocabulary, etc.);
- time gap between strategy use and data collection;
- researcher and participant training in the use of the method;
- the number of participants and researchers;
- resources available;
- context of the research (L2, FL).

Future research should include further testing and improvement of research methods or their combinations in different research contexts. In any case, a wide range of available methods and the possibility of data triangulation are the advantages that research on L2 learning strategies should benefit from.

Notes

1. Nation (2001) states that the keyword method studies exceed 100. For a more detailed survey see Hulstijn (2000).
2. The studies were conducted on Italian as a FL in Australia.
3. cf. study conducted by Gu and Johnson (1996) that revealed that the Chinese learners use strategies based on meaning more frequently than those based on mechanical repetition.
4. SCANR is a strategy for inferencing a new word's meaning from context, developed by Jenkins *et al.* (1989). Its name, SCANR, is an abbreviation based on the initial letters of words denoting the order of the procedure: substitute (a new word with another word or expression), check (for keys in the context to confirm the assumption), ask (if the substitute corresponds to all keys from the context), need (for a new idea?), revise (the assumption according to the context).
5. 'Chinese learners employ more rote learning strategies, the caricature of Asians so often seen in the literature, than other "better" strategies endorsed by North American researchers...' (Gu & Johnson, 1996: 644).
6. The distinction between Discovery and Consolidation strategies was taken over from Cook and Mayer (1983) and Nation (1990).
7. Still, evidence emanating from some later empirical research (cf. Hsiao & Oxford, 2002) runs counter to this conclusion.

8. Cohen (1998), for example, reports on a host of workshops on how to learn held at the Minnesota University during the academic year 1994/95, one of which was devoted to vocabulary learning. In addition to receiving information on theoretical and empirical foundations, the students participated in practical activities for practising general and specific learning strategies and in discussions on ways of improving their strategy use, the problems they encounter in learning, transfer of strategies to new tasks, etc.

Chapter 4

Studies on Vocabulary Learning Strategies

This chapter will report on three studies of vocabulary learning strategies used by elementary school learners of English as a foreign language. The first study focused on the development of a reliable and valid instrument for measuring the frequency of vocabulary learning strategy use. It also attempted to classify the vocabulary learning strategies. The second study explored the relationship between vocabulary teaching and vocabulary learning strategies. The third study set out to investigate the differences in the strategic approach to vocabulary learning by learners of two different foreign languages.

Study 1: Designing a Vocabulary Learning Strategy Questionnaire

Introduction

Collecting data by means of questionnaires is not an uncommon research method in the field of language learning strategies (LLS). However, only a few validated instruments measuring the frequency of LLS use currently exist. Certainly, the most popular one is the *SILL* (Oxford, 1990), which has been validated across cultures and languages. *SILL* is generic and extensive, and it is in English, which necessitates validated translated versions if it is to be applied with speakers of other languages. Chamot (2001), among other scholars, suggested creating an instrument for measuring the use of LLS that would need to correspond to the research context and the dimensions defining it, such as learners' age and developmental stages, because using adequate tools for collecting the necessary data, i.e. 'the tools that will serve the purposes of [the] particular project' (Brown, 2001: 8) is a precondition of any fruitful research study. The need to create a questionnaire focusing on the use of a specific set of LLS and addressing a target population is further justified by the fact that LLS are idiosyncratic and that their choice is affected by a number of factors.

This study was conducted with the aim of constructing a questionnaire for measuring the use of a specific set of LLS, namely the vocabulary learning strategies (hereafter VLS) in the context defined by the following two dimensions: (1) FL (as opposed to L2) learning and (2) learner level and age (primary school learners, aged between 10 and 14). The study will focus on examining some psychometric properties of the questionnaire, primarily its construct validity (by means of factor analysis) and internal consistency reliability (Cronbach's α).

Phase I

In Phase I a two-part questionnaire was developed: the first part consisted of questions addressing demographic information (age, gender, etc.) and the second part referred to questions about the learners' use of VLS.

The aim of the first part of the questionnaire was to gather information useful for describing learners in some detail (age, gender, class, school, achievement).

The second part of the questionnaire targeting VLS use was designed on the basis of the questionnaire used in a previous study (Pavičić, 1999). A few statements were modified to some degree in order to make their formulation more precise or to make them understandable to primary school learners (e.g. statements number 36, 37, 44, 46 and 49; see Appendix A). The questionnaire was expanded by adding VLS generated by the aforementioned previous study (Pavičić, 1999), and by adding VLS which needed to be explored (e.g. VLS involving the use of computers and the Internet). The expanded version of the questionnaire consisted of a total of 69 statements targeting learners' use of VLS. The statements were followed by a three-point scale (where 1 meant 'never', 2 'sometimes' and 3 'always). It was believed that a three-point scale was more suitable for the primary school level and would give more valid responses.

Before administering the questionnaire, the researcher conducted a focus group discussion in which three primary school learners (aged 13) took part. The aim was to ensure the content and face validity of the questionnaire. The learners, chosen at random by their teacher, were asked to study both parts of the questionnaire in detail and comment on the wording of the instructions and statements, as well as the layout, and to suggest any changes that would make the questionnaire clear to learners of their age. On the one hand, the discussion revealed that the learners were familiar with most of the technical terms (e.g. context, definition, synonym) used in the questionnaire and that they were able to explain their meaning. On the other hand, certain changes were requested, and as a result of the talk, some statements were modified by paraphrasing or simplifying (e.g. pilot statement 9), adding examples (e.g. pilot statement 3) or by highlighting a part of the statement (e.g. pilot statement 4). Also, the order of the statements was changed to avoid confusion. Interestingly, the learners were not able to understand fully the statement referring to the use of the Keyword Method or confused it with the strategy of noticing cognates. This fact, as well as some research findings (Avila & Sadoski, 1996; Pavičić, 1999) suggesting that the spontaneous use of the Keyword Method is extremely rare or only used by trained learners, led to the conclusion that this strategy should be excluded from the questionnaire.

Phase II: Pilot study

Methodology

Participants. The participants in the study were chosen to serve the purpose of the study, i.e. to resemble the sample to be used in the main study. A total of 99 primary school learners of three different levels (6th, 7th and 8th grade) and from three different schools (a town school, a suburban school and a village school) participated in the study.

Materials. The questionnaire used in the study is included as Appendix A. The pilot version, revised on the basis of the focus group discussion described earlier, consisted of two parts. The first part of the questionnaire assessed learners' background factors. The second part, containing 69 items, targeted learners' use of vocabulary learning strategies. They were to record their responses on the same three-point Likert scale.

Procedure. According to standard procedure, after introducing the researcher, the teacher would leave the classroom. The researcher explained the purpose of the study and the way in which the questionnaire should be filled in. It was made clear to the participants that the survey was anonymous, that no answer would be considered incorrect, that the results would be used only for the purposes of the research, and that, therefore, they should answer the questions honestly. The participants were encouraged to ask for help or additional explanations if needed. It took learners between 20 and 45 minutes to complete the questionnaire.

Results of the pilot study

The demographic data collected were not statistically analysed, but they were examined in order to determine whether the questions were well formulated, how long it would take to complete the questionnaire and whether the answers could be appropriately coded for statistical analyses.

In analysing the data on VLS statistically, SPSS for Windows 8.0 was used. Several factor analyses were conducted in order to refine the questionnaire items and reduce their number to a more manageable number of variables (see Appendix C). Also, factor analyses were used to identify the underlying, not-directly-observable constructs based on the set of observable variables. The basic assumption was that by identifying a relatively small number of factors it would be possible to explain complex relationships among sets of interrelated variables. In addition, a reliability analysis was conducted, i.e. the scales' internal consistency was measured. Cronbach's alpha coefficient was used as the indicator of internal consistency. Alpha equal to or greater than 0.7 was considered satisfactory.

The approach used in factor extraction was principal component analysis (eigenvalues > 1). Varimax rotation (using Kaiser normalisation) was performed to aid in the interpretation of the components. Table 4.1. shows the rotated matrix of the final two factor solution where only loadings greater than 0.4 were retained.

The interpretation of the three components revealed that the strategies for incidental vocabulary learning (primarily from the mass media), strategies for active and communicative vocabulary use, as well as memory strategies based on affect loaded strongly on Component 1. Strategies for systematic vocabulary learning and revision, including social VLS, loaded strongly on Component 2. Memory strategies, many of which include the visual support in learning, strategies for practising as well as exposure to the target language loaded strongly on Component 3.

All three subscales had good internal consistency, with a Cronbach's alpha coefficient above 0.7.

Conclusion of the pilot study

On the basis of the results of the statistical analyses it was concluded that the questionnaire should be further investigated. One of the reasons was that the total number of questionnaire items per participant was quite extensive. Therefore, it was considered necessary to administer the questionnaire to a larger sample, after which a new factor analysis, interpretation of the components and reliability analyses of the subscales

Table 4.1 Varimax rotation of three-factor solution for reduced pVLS items (pilot study)

Variable		Components			h^2
		1	2	3	
pVLS5	Remembering words from films and TV programmes	0.618			0.685
pVLS41	Multiple encounters with a word	0.595			0.726
pVLS61	Affective associations	0.551			0.721
pVLS35	Using circumlocution	0.503			0.588
pVLS33	Remembering 'complicated' words	0.493			0.701
pVLS48	Remembering words from books, magazines, etc.	0.471			0.756
pVLS6	Using known words in new contexts	0.460			0.595
pVLS54	Remembering words from computer games	0.439			0.825
pVLS69	Remembering words from the Internet	0.414			0.751
pVLS56	Associating words with personal experience	0.406			0.652
pVLS43	Using new words in speaking or writing	0.404			0.668
pVLS23	Repeating new words aloud when studying		0.605		0.856
pVLS3	Regular reviewing outside classroom		0.553		0.683
pVLS55	Getting help in conversations		0.539		0.798
pVLS20	Planning for vocabulary learning		0.538		0.745

Table 4.1 (*Continued*)

| Variable | | Components | | h^2 |
	1	2	3	
pVLS30	Asking someone for meaning		0.511		0.729
pVLS44	Repeating words mentally		0.498		0.708
pVLS59	Getting someone to test the knowledge		0.469		0.673
pVLS67	Testing oneself with word lists		0.467		0.765
pVLS4	Testing oneself		0.406		0.722
pVLS24	Imaging word's meaning			0.685	0.760
pVLS34	Imaging word's orthographical form			0.571	0.719
pVLS29	Taking notes when watching films and TV programmes			0.539	0.780
pVLS58	Connecting words with physical objects			0.533	0.609
pVLS45	Guessing from context			0.521	0.712
pVLS39	Grouping words together to study them			0.518	0.736
pVLS1	Using new words in sentences			0.517	0.623
pVLS42	Use physical action when learning a word			0.451	0.743
pVLS18	Making word cards			0.424	0.615
pVLS8	Associating words with their position on page			0.408	0.723

Table 4.1 (*Continued*)

Variable		Components			h^2
		1	*2*	*3*	
pVLS64	Practising with friends			0.407	0.805
	% of variance explained	13.759	7.488	5.796	
	Cumulative%	13.759	21.247	27.043	
	Cronbach's α	0.7243	0.7476	0.7274	

h^2, communality

should be performed. As a result of the factor analyses, the initial list of items in the questionnaire was reduced to 53 statements to be included in the main study (marked with an asterisk in Appendix A). Also, it had been noticed that participants tended to lose concentration in the course of filling in the questionnaire, so it was decided to alter the order of questionnaire parts: the part on the use of VLS, as more demanding, was the first part, followed by background information.

Phase III: Main study

Methodology

Participants. The study targeted the population of primary school learners of English as a FL. A total of 358 learners from 17 classes and eight different schools participated in the study. The sample consisted of 180 female (50.3%) and 173 (48.3%) male learners (5 learners did not state their gender). The participants attended 6th, 7th and 8th grade of primary school. There were 139 eighth-graders (38.8%), 116 (32.4%) sixth-graders and 103 (28.8%) seventh-graders.

Materials. The 53-item questionnaire on VLS use was used in this study (Appendix A). The second part of the questionnaire contained questions on learners' demographic characteristics.

Procedure. The procedure followed was the same as in the Pilot Study. Again, after introducing the researcher, the teacher left the classroom. The researcher explained the purpose of the study and gave instructions for filling in the questionnaire. It was emphasised that the survey was anonymous, that there were no incorrect answers and that the results would not be revealed. The participants were also invited to ask for help or additional explanations if necessary. It took learners up to 40 minutes to complete the questionnaire.

Results

Several factor analyses were conducted (principal components analysis, eigenvalues > 1). Table 4.2 shows the initial statistics and Table 4.3 the rotated solution. As can be seen in Table 4.3, 27 items were extracted and the three components explained 38.24% of the total variance, with the first component, which showed the strongest loadings, contributing 22.13%, the second 9.64% and the third 6.46%.

The rotated solutions could be clearly and consistently interpreted. As the rotated solution (see Table 4.3) revealed, all three components have strong loadings, with the second component containing a larger number of variables. The solution can be interpreted as follows: component 1 was

Table 4.2 Initial statistics for VLS items (main study)

Component	Eigenvalue	%Variance	Cumulative%
1	5.977	22.136	22.136
2	2.605	9.647	31.783
3	1.744	6.458	38.240
4	1.376	5.097	43.338
5	1.083	4.009	47.347
6	1.030	3.815	51.163
7	0.965	3.575	54.737
8	0.923	3.417	58.154
9	0.880	3.259	61.413
10	0.844	3.126	64.540
11	0.828	3.067	67.606
12	0.772	2.861	70.467
13	0.716	2.653	73.120
14	0.698	2.586	75.706
15	0.679	2.514	78.221
16	0.622	2.302	80.523
17	0.611	2.262	82.785
18	0.604	2.236	85.021
19	0.567	2.100	87.121
20	0.546	2.021	89.142
21	0.497	1.839	90.981
22	0.474	1.756	92.737
23	0.459	1.698	94.435
24	0.413	1.528	95.964
25	0.386	1.429	97.393

Table 4.2 (*Continued*)

Component	Eigenvalue	% Variance	Cumulative%
26	0.375	1.387	98.780
27	0.329	1.220	100.000

labelled FORMAL VOCABULARY LEARNING and identified as a subscale encompassing strategies of rote vocabulary memorisation, reliance on L1, and a metacognitive aspect of regular and planned revision; component 2 was labelled INDEPENDENT VOCABULARY LEARNING and includes the strategies of exposure to the target language and those strategies that reveal an elaborated approach to vocabulary study that includes the use of memory strategies; component 3 was labelled INCIDENTAL VOCABULARY LEARNING and contains strategies of spontaneous vocabulary learning in naturalistic learning situations as well as communication strategies.

To test the reliability, the internal consistency of each subscale as well as of the total scale was assessed by Cronbach's alpha coefficient. Internal consistency of the subscales was 0.73 to 0.82 and Cronbach's alpha for the total scale was 0.83 (see Table 4.3).

Discussion

In the framework of the statistical analysis several factor analyses were conducted on the variables referring to VLS. The initial inventory was honed to 27 items. The low percentage of the total variance explained indicates that there is a number of factors in addition to VLS which influence the process of learning vocabulary in the FL.

The interpretations of the rotated solutions revealed three components referring to three different aspects of vocabulary learning. The interpretations of rotated solutions were meaningful and generally consistent, which leads to the conclusion that previously proposed classifications of VLS cannot be applied (cf. Oxford, 1990, *passim*; Kudo, 1999), but that a new classification of VLS can be proposed:

(1) STRATEGIES OF FORMAL VOCABULARY LEARNING AND PRACTISING;
(2) SELF-INITIATED INDEPENDENT VOCABULARY LEARNING;
(3) SPONTANEOUS (INCIDENTAL) VOCABULARY LEARNING (ACQUISITION).

Table 4.3 Final factor structure of the VOLSQES using principal component analysis with Varimax rotation (27 items)

Variable		*Component*			h^2
		1	2	3	
VLS10	Repeating new words aloud when studying	0.730			0.571
VLS21	Repeating words mentally	0.657			0.468
VLS14	Writing down words repeatedly to remember them	0.616			0.449
VLS4	Testing oneself	0.583			0.397
VLS26	Testing oneself with word lists	0.557			0.382
VLS3	Regular reviewing outside classroom	0.541			0.393
VLS9	Remembering words if they are written down	0.534			0.323
VLS8	Planning for vocabulary learning	0.526			0.378
VLS2	Making word lists	0.523			0.307
VLS24	Using spaced word practice	0.517			0.262
VLS19	Translating words into L1	0.498			0.312
VLS13	Taking notes when watching films and TV programmes		0.662		0.445
VLS7	Taking notes while reading for pleasure		0.617		0.395
VLS16	Imaging word's orthographical form		0.589		0.437

Table 4.3 (*Continued*)

Variable		Component			h^2
		1	2	3	
VLS20	Grouping words together to study them		0.585		0.375
VLS25	Connecting words to physical objects		0.563		0.369
VLS11	Imaging word's meaning		0.523		0.384
VLS18	Associating words with the context		0.522		0.334
VLS15	Reading and leafing through dictionary		0.503		0.301
VLS1	Using new words in sentences		0.479		0.271
VLS23	Remembering words from books, magazines			0.646	0.470
VLS17	Using circumlocution			0.639	0.427
VLS22	Listening to songs in target language			0.632	0.434
VLS27	Remembering words from the Internet			0.614	0.414
VLS12	Associating new words with already known			0.598	0.410
VLS6	Using synonyms in conversations			0.543	0.301
VLS5	Remembering words from films and TV programmes			0.541	0.315
	% of variance explained	22.136	9.647	6.458	
	Cumulative%	22.136	31.783	38.240	

Table 4.3 (*Continued*)

Variable		Component			h^2
		1	2	3	
	Cronbach's α	0.8255	0.7762	0.7311	
	Mean	2.093	1.615	2.282	

h^2, communality

The first set of strategies is made up of VLS employed in learning a FL in a formal (classroom-based) context. Their use is based on instrumental motivation and is oriented towards concrete formal language learning tasks. For example, learners will repeat lexical items and test themselves, often using a list of words and their translations, because they expect their teachers to test them in the same way. In other words, learners will opt for those VLS which would help them meet the requirements of instructed language learning or to attain their personal goal, such as getting a satisfactory mark. In contrast to some previous studies (Nyikos & Oxford, 1993), the factor analysis did not reveal the existence of functional VLS. This can probably be attributed to the fact that the study was conducted in the context of learning English as a foreign (not second) language, where there is no real need for communication in the target language. In such a context, the third set of VLS seems to be of vital importance, for it is characterised by exposure to the target language outside the language classroom which does not include a conscious effort to learn. By using such VLS, learners may undergo the process of acquiring, rather than learning, lexical items. As learners use them outside the classroom, their use is probably dependent on learners' personal interests. The second set of VLS (self-initiated independent vocabulary learning) is characterised by a more systematic approach to vocabulary learning, i.e. by conscious efforts that learners make in order to learn lexical items. For examples of individual VLS in each category, see Table 4.3.

Internal consistency of the subscales as well as of the total scale was judged acceptable.

Conclusion

Overall, the main study showed promising results, for it yielded an instrument that should be considered valid and reliable in measuring the frequency of VLS use and that is simple enough to administer to elementary school learners. After several factor analyses and reinterpretations the initial VLS inventory was reduced to 27 items and named *Vocabulary Learning Strategy Questionnaire for Elementary Schools (VOLSQES)* (see Appendix B). Finally, by proposing a tentative classification of vocabulary learning strategies this study makes an important contribution to a better understanding of the nature and purpose of VLS.

It should be recognised, however, that this study has some limitations that warrant further investigation. To note but one, further and more detailed psychometric testing of the questionnaire should be performed possibly including a broader age range of primary school learners.

Study 2: The Relationship Between Vocabulary Learning Strategies and Vocabulary Teaching Strategies

Introduction: The context of the study

Over the last three decades there has been intensive interest in research on LLS as a result of the efforts made by language educators to enhance the role of the individual learner in the language learning process. Many of these studies have explored the patterns of relationships between LLS and one or more linguistic and non-linguistic factors such as age, sex, motivation, personality traits, profession, ethnic and cultural background, language task, etc. (see Chapter 3). However, the role of *teaching* strategies in the development and selection of learning strategies has been neglected, despite the fact that many researchers have recognised and emphasised the need to include this variable in their studies. For example, O'Malley and Chamot (1996) report on a study whose results implied that learners may select their LLS under the direct influence of teaching strategies employed by their teachers. Similarly, the language task, i.e. its nature and requirements, may play a critical role in the selection of LLS.

The above-mentioned conclusions inspired the present study, which is aimed at exploring in greater detail the relationship between the strategies of learning and the strategies of teaching vocabulary in a FL.

The general approach adopted is basically the social constructivist (cf. Williams & Burden, 2001). The social constructivist approach emphasises the dynamic nature of the interplay among the following key sets of factors:

- teacher
- learner
- task
- context.

Teachers select tasks according to their own beliefs about teaching and learning. Learners interpret these tasks in their own way. Therefore, the task is the interface between teachers and learners. The task as one of the set of factors includes learning materials. The interaction between learners and teachers reflects teachers' beliefs and values and learners' individual characteristics (e.g. their problem solving ability) that they bring into the learning context. The teacher, learner and task, as Williams and Burden (2001) explain, are a dynamic equilibrium. The context in which the learning takes place refers to the immediate emotional and physical environment, as well as to the wider social, political and cultural context. A change in any set of the factors has a bearing on other factors: if, for example, a teacher changes the coursebook, the balance among all factors will be affected.

In the present study, the learning situation is defined by all of the aforementioned factors with a view to create a complete picture of the interaction between vocabulary learning strategies and vocabulary teaching strategies in teaching English as a FL.

The learner is conceived of as the central factor in the learning situation defined by a set of demographic data (e.g. age, gender, language learning experience, etc.), and by the vocabulary learning strategies he or she uses in and outside the language classroom. *Vocabulary learning strategies* are activities, behaviours, steps or techniques used by learners (often deliberately) to facilitate vocabulary learning. Vocabulary learning strategies can help learners to discover lexical items (both their meaning and form), and to internalise, store, retrieve and actively use these in language production.

In a social constructivist view, all individuals construct their reality in their own way, even in what may seem as similar conditions. In other words, learners perceive and interpret the learning and teaching situation in different ways. Therefore, in the present study there is an additional dimension which defines the learner, and that is his or her *perception* of vocabulary teaching strategies.

The teacher is defined by the vocabulary teaching strategies he or she uses. *Vocabulary teaching strategies* refer to everything teachers do or should do in order to help learners learn the vocabulary of the target language (Hatch & Brown, 2000). These would include the following procedures: introducing and presenting the meaning and form of a lexical item, stimulating learners to revise, practice and consolidate, i.e. recycle vocabulary through various tasks, as well as other procedures related to vocabulary teaching, such as giving advice to learners on how to memorise lexical items, monitoring, and evaluating learners' progress.

The task generally refers to vocabulary learning and acquisition, but also encompasses the tasks set by teaching and learning materials, i.e. the learners' coursebook and workbook, which often serve as a framework for selection of teaching strategies.

The learning context is determined by teaching conditions in terms of the composition of learner groups (number, proficiency level), location (classroom) and time (duration and frequency of language classes). In its wider sense, the context is defined by English as the learners' FL and Croatian as their L1.

Research questions

The overall aim of the study was to determine the relationship between vocabulary learning strategies and vocabulary teaching strategies, i.e. the relationship between the teaching process and development and application of (EFL) vocabulary learning strategies. Thus, the main research question (RQ1) was whether there is a difference in VLS usage between a group of learners whose teachers use a corresponding VTS and those learners whose teachers do not use it. It was hypothesised that there is a connection between the usage of VLS used by primary school learners and VTS used by their teachers. In other words, it was assumed that the implementation of a certain VTS would bring about the use of a corresponding VLS. In line with the social constructivist approach adopted in the study, it was assumed that the selection of VLS might also be influenced by the learners' perception of VTS. The second research question (RQ2) was whether there is a difference between VTS as perceived by learners and their use of VLS.

Before exploring the two main research questions it was necessary to find out the following:

- what vocabulary learning strategies are used by elementary learners of English;
- what is the learners' perception of VTS used by their teachers;
- what vocabulary teaching strategies are employed by teachers, i.e. what presentation strategies are used when vocabulary is introduced, and what types of tasks and exercises are chosen for vocabulary revision and consolidation; and
- what vocabulary teaching strategies are included in the learning materials.

Methods

Along the lines of recommendations and conclusions reached in previous research (see Chapter 3), in order to make research results more credible and to illuminate the research in question, triangulation was used which included the following:

- data triangulation (using multiple sources of information, i.e. teachers and learners);
- investigator triangulation (using multiple researchers in transcript analysis);
- methodological triangulation (using multiple data-gathering procedures, i.e. questionnaires, observations and textbook analysis);

- location triangulation (using multiple data-gathering sites, i.e. multiple schools).

Participants

The target population in the study involved primary school learners in Croatia. As the results of various previous studies suggested that early adolescence is the most favourable age for FL learning (McLaughlin, 1987: 29), it can be assumed that learners of this age are susceptible to interventions, i.e. that development of their learning strategies can be more effectively influenced.

The study was carried out in eight primary schools. Altogether 9 teachers and 17 primary school classes (Grades 6, 7 and 8)[1] were involved. The questionnaire was administered to a total of 358 participants (180 female and 173 male learners) aged 12–15. There were 139 (38.8%) 8th-graders, 103 (28.8%) 7th-graders and 116 (32.4%) 6th-graders. They had been learning English as a first FL for five years on average. The learners in the sample had been taught by the same teacher for 2.7 years on average.

Classroom video recordings were obtained by videotaping five consecutive English lessons in nine classes (one class per teacher). A total of 45 lessons were recorded. Learning materials used as a source of information on vocabulary learning strategies were selected on the basis of teachers' statements.

Materials

The main instrument of this study was the questionnaire. Its principal part, *VOLSQES*, was used to assess the frequency of VLS usage. It consisted of 27 items in the form of statements followed by a three-point scale (where 0 meant 'never', 1 'sometimes' and 3 'always'). The questionnaire's internal consistency reliability was measured using Cronbach's alpha at 0.89 for this sample.

The supplementary part of the questionnaire contained a scale of 29 statements about learners' perception of vocabulary teaching strategies ($\alpha = 0.82$), and questions eliciting basic background information about learners (see Appendix B).

The data on VTS were obtained by analysing two sources:

(1) The transcripts of a total of 45 classroom lessons. These were compiled by videotaping five consecutive lessons each lasting for 45 minutes in every class. The transcripts were coded by the researcher and another independent coder. The intercoder agreement coefficient was 85% (Table 4.4). It is important to emphasise that the

Table 4.4 Intercoder agreement coefficient

	1. Coding		2. Coding	
	Number of codings that agree	*Total number of codings*	*Number of codings that agree*	*Total number of codings*
Teacher 1	29	54	25	25
Teacher 2	27	58	29	31
Teacher 3	23	45	17	22
Teacher 4	30	56	23	26
Teacher 5	23	53	23	30
Teacher 6	38	61	16	23
Teacher 7	20	45	20	25
Teacher 8	14	31	16	17
Teacher 9	20	42	18	22
Total	224	445	187	221
Agreement coefficient		50.33%		85%

purpose of classroom transcript analysis was not to assess the *quality* of teaching strategies, but to determine whether a teaching strategy is present or not.

(2) As it was assumed that the choice of teaching strategies is often based on tasks provided by learning materials, it was necessary to analyse the learning materials (i.e. learners' textbooks and workbooks) used in order to gain a better insight into vocabulary teaching procedures. Six different sets of materials were analysed (Breka, 2001; Breka & Mardešić, 2001; Džeba & Mardešić, 2001; Jagatić, 1997, 2000; Mavar *et al.*, 2000).

In this way, dichotomous variables (0 = VTS absent; 1 = VTS present) were obtained to be included in the further analysis.

The analysis of both transcripts and learning materials was conducted according to the criteria established in advance on the basis of literature inspection (see Appendix D).

Procedure

The study was conducted following a predetermined order: first the data on vocabulary teaching strategies were collected by videotaping English lessons in order to avoid influencing the teachers' selection of vocabulary teaching strategies. Also, the main purpose of the study had not been revealed to the teachers or learners in advance. The classes in which the lessons were videotaped were selected by the teachers. No negative reactions were noticed during videotaping.

After the videotaping was completed, the researcher administered the questionnaire to the learners.

Results

The results of tapescript and learning materials analyses are shown in Appendix D. Table 4.5 shows the frequency distribution of VLS used (mean as the indicator of central tendency).

The data collected were statistically analysed. A database containing four sets of variables was formed. The first variable set encompassed VLS used by learners, the second was made up of learners' perception of VTS, the third referred to VTS and the fourth set entailed demographic information on learners.

In order to determine whether there is a difference in VLS use related to VTS, a *t*-test was used. It is a statistical procedure used when comparing the mean score on a continuous variable (i.e. VLS use) for two different groups of subjects (defined by absence or presence of a

Table 4.5 Frequency distribution of VLS items (criterion: Mean) (*N* = 358)

Variable		*N*	*Min.*	*Max.*	*Mean*	*Std. deviation*
VLS22	Listening to songs in target language	358	1.00	3.00	2.6034	0.6771
VLS5	Remembering words from films and TV programmes	358	1.00	3.00	2.5726	0.6072
VLS19	Translating words into L1	357	1.00	3.00	2.5658	0.5942
VLS9	Remembering words if they are written down	358	1.00	3.00	2.4637	0.6058
VLS6	Using synonyms in conversations	358	1.00	3.00	2.3128	0.6673
VLS10	Repeating new words aloud when studying	358	1.00	3.00	2.2514	0.7245
VLS21	Repeating words mentally	358	1.00	3.00	2.2291	0.7203
VLS26	Testing oneself with word lists	358	1.00	3.00	2.2067	0.7863
VLS23	Remembering words from books, magazines	358	1.00	3.00	2.2067	0.7270
VLS17	Using circumlocution	356	1.00	3.00	2.1573	0.7105
VLS12	Associating new words with already known	357	1.00	3.00	2.1317	0.6927
VLS4	Testing oneself	358	1.00	3.00	2.0279	0.7095
VLS2	Making word lists	358	1.00	3.00	2.0168	0.7848
VLS27	Remembering words from the Internet	356	1.00	3.00	1.9944	0.8084
VLS11	Imaging word's meaning	358	1.00	3.00	1.8631	0.7067
VLS3	Regular reviewing outside classroom	358	1.00	3.00	1.8547	0.7030

Table 4.5 (*Continued*)

Variable	N	Min.	Max.	Mean	Std. deviation
VLS24	Using spaced word practice	357	1.00	3.00	1.8403	0.7109
VLS14	Writing down words repeatedly to remember them	358	1.00	3.00	1.8324	0.7521
VLS1	Using new words in sentences	358	1.00	3.00	1.8296	0.6408
VLS25	Connecting words to physical objects	357	1.00	3.00	1.8179	0.6974
VLS8	Planning for vocabulary learning	358	1.00	3.00	1.7346	0.7097
VLS18	Associating words with the context	358	1.00	3.00	1.7318	0.6132
VLS15	Reading and leafing through dictionary	357	1.00	3.00	1.7031	0.7121
VLS16	Imaging word's orthographical form	358	1.00	3.00	1.6927	0.6443
VLS20	Grouping words together to study them	357	1.00	3.00	1.3669	0.5780
VLS7	Taking notes while reading for pleasure	357	1.00	3.00	1.3333	0.5692
VLS13	Taking notes when watching films and TV programmes	358	1.00	3.00	1.2011	0.4599
Valid N (listwise)		347				

VTS) (Hair *et al.*, 1998; Pallant, 2001). Mutually compatible VLS and teaching strategies were compared, for example, VLS1 (*Using new words in sentences*) was compared to two teaching strategies: VTS 55 (*Task: completing a sentence*) and VTS75 (*Task: use new words in sentences*); VLS 6 (*Using synonyms in conversations*) was compared to four different teaching strategies that were considered compatible: VTS2g (*Writing synonyms on board*), VTS3b (*Listing synonyms*), VTS22 (*Presenting meaning through synonyms*) and VTS51 (*Task: give synonyms*); and so on. Altogether, 31 variables were tested. The results are shown in Table 4.6.

An alternative hypothesis was put forward stating that learners whose teachers apply a compatible VTS will use a VLS more often than the learners whose teachers do not. The results of the *t*-test showed that there was a statistically significant difference at the $p < 0.05$ level for the following variables:

- VLS6 Using synonyms in conversations compared to VTS2g *Writing synonyms on board* (t = − 1.991, df = 356, p = − 0.047),
- VLS6 Using synonyms in conversations compared to VTS3b *Listing synonyms* (t = − 2.240, df = 356, p = − 0.026),
- VLS15 Reading and leafing through dictionary compared to VTS73 *Check meaning in dictionary* (t = − 2.179, df = 355, p = 0.030),
- VLS17 *Using circumlocution* compared to VTS62 *Explain words in English* (t = − 2.183, df = 354, p = 0.030).

At the $p < 0.01$ level, *t*-test indicated a statistically significant difference for one variable:

- VLS11 *Imaging the word's meaning* compared to VTS24 Presenting meaning *using pictures* (t = − 3.238, df = 356, p = 0.001).

For these five variables, the alternative hypothesis, namely that there is an association between learners' use of VLS and teachers' VTS, can be accepted.

In order to assess the strength of association, the effect size was calculated using η^2 (see Table 4.7). The guidelines for interpreting these values are: 0.01 = small effect, 0.06 = moderate effect and 0.14 = large effect. So, despite reaching statistical significance, the actual difference in mean scores was quite small.

On the other hand, the alternative hypothesis that there is a connection between VLS and VTS can be rejected for the majority of variables (84%). For these variables, the null hypothesis implying the independence of VLS usage of VTS employed by teachers can be accepted.

Table 4.6 Comparison of mean scores for VTS and VLS (independent samples *t*-test)

Variable		Mean values and standard deviations (for VTS)		*t-test*	*Sig.*
		0 absent	*1 present*		
VLS1 (VTS55)	*n*	44	314	−0.628	0.530
	Mean	1.7727	1.8376		
	δ	0.6773	0.6368		
VLS4 (VTS5)	*n*	228	130	−0.831	0.406
	Mean	2.0044	2.0692		
	δ	0.7240	0.6841		
VLS6 (VTS2g)	*n*	319	39	−1.991	0.047*
	Mean	2.2884	2.5128		
	δ	0.6716	0.6013		
VLS6 (VTS3b)	*n*	176	182	−2.240	0.026*
	Mean	2.2330	2.3901		
	δ	0.6737	0.6535		
VLS6 (VTS22)	*n*	79	279	−0.518	0.605
	Mean	2.2785	2.3226		
	δ	0.6392	0.6758		

Table 4.6 (*Continued*)

Variable		Mean values and standard deviations (for VTS)		t-test	Sig.
		0 absent	1 present		
VLS6 (VTS51)	n	72	286	0.291	0.771
	Mean	2.3333	2.3077		
	δ	0.6500	0.6725		
VLS9 (VTS46a)	n	328	30	0.286	0.775
	Mean	2.4665	2.4333		
	δ	0.6098	0.5683		
VLS9 (VTS46c)	n	154	204	−1.130	0.259
	Mean	2.4221	2.4951		
	δ	0.6133	0.5996		
VLS9 (VTS2a)	n	93	265	0.373	0.709
	Mean	2.4839	2.4566		
	δ	0.6009	0.6085		
VLS9 (VTS2b)	n	178	180	−0.093	0.926
	Mean	2.4607	2.4667		
	δ	0.6208	0.5923		

Table 4.6 (*Continued*)

Variable		Mean values and standard deviations (for VTS)		t-test	Sig.
		0 absent	1 present		
VLS10 (VTS58)	n	37	321	0.407	0.685
	Mean	2.2973	2.2461		
	δ	0.7403	0.7236		
VLS10 (VTS6)	n	79	279	0.552	0.581
	Mean	2.2911	2.2401		
	δ	0.7364	0.7219		
VLS11 (VTS15)	n	328	30	− 0.568	0.570
	Mean	1.8567	1.9333		
	δ	0.6957	0.8276		
VLS11 (VTS24)	n	90	268	− 3.238	0.001**
	Mean	1.6556	1.9328		
	δ	0.7057	0.6945		
VLS12 (VTS11)	n	244	113	− 1.501	0.134
	Mean	2.0943	2.2124		
	δ	0.7051	0.6607		

Table 4.6 (*Continued*)

Variable		Mean values and standard deviations (for VTS)		t-test	Sig.
		0 absent	1 present		
VLS15 (VTS41)	n	290	67	1.354	0.177
	Mean	1.7276	1.5970		
	δ	0.7143	0.6976		
VLS15 (VTS73)	n	30	327	−2.179	0.030*
	Mean	1.4333	1.7278		
	δ	0.6260	0.7152		
VLS16 (VTS2a)	n	93	265	−1.015	0.311
	Mean	1.6344	1.7132		
	δ	0.6218	0.6519		
VLS16 (VTS2b)	n	178	180	−1.695	0.091
	Mean	1.6348	1.7500		
	δ	0.6345	0.6505		
VLS16 (VTS46a)	n	328	30	0.823	0.411
	Mean	1.7012	1.6000		
	δ	0.7240	0.6841		

Table 4.6 (Continued)

Variable		Mean values and standard deviations (for VTS)		t-test	Sig.
		0 absent	1 present		
VLS17 (VTS62)	n	103	253	−2.183	0.030*
	Mean	2.0291	2.2095		
	δ	0.7065	0.7068		
VLS18 (VTS10d)	n	120	238	−1.430	0.154
	Mean	1.6667	1.7647		
	δ	0.5987	0.6190		
VLS18 (VTS61)	n	328	30	0.608	0.544
	Mean	1.7378	1.6667		
	δ	0.6044	0.7111		
VLS19 (VTS2c)	n	214	143	−0.711	0.478
	Mean	2.5841	2.5385		
	δ	0.5893	0.6024		
VLS19 (VTS5b)	n	313	44	−1.112	0.267
	Mean	2.5527	2.6591		
	δ	0.5974	0.5682		

Table 4.6 (*Continued*)

Variable		Mean values and standard deviations (for VTS)		t-test	Sig.
		0 absent	1 present		
VLS19 (VTS5c)	n	265	92	− 1.492	0.137
	Mean	2.5396	2.6413		
	δ	0.6088	0.5463		
VLS19 (VTS10i)	n	270	87	0.047	0.963
	Mean	2.5667	2.56322		
	δ	0.5857	0.6232		
VLS19 (VTS18)	n	117	240	− 1.868	0.063
	Mean	2.4786	2.6083		
	δ	0.6379	0.5683		
VLS25 (VTS69b)	n	308	49	− 1.370	0.175
	Mean	1.7987	1.9388		
	δ	0.7025	0.6585		
VLS26 (VTS5b)	n	314	44	− 0.799	0.425
	Mean	2.1943	2.2955		
	δ	0.7814	0.8234		

Table 4.6 (*Continued*)

Variable			Mean values and standard deviations (for VTS)		t-test	Sig.
			0 absent	*1 present*		
VLS26 (VTS5c)		*n*	265	93	− 1.347	0.179
	Mean		2.1736	2.3011		
	δ		0.7882	0.7771		

$*p < 0.05$
$**p < 0.01$

Table 4.7 Analysis of the size effect for the independent-samples *t*-test (VLS and VTS)

Variable	η^2
VLS6 (VTS2g)	0.01
VLS6 (VTS3b)	0.01
VLS11 (VTS24)	0.03
VLS15 (VTS73)	0.01
VLS17 (VTS62)	0.01

Finally, in order to investigate the relationship between learners' perception of VTS and their use of VLS, Paired-Samples *t*-test was run. Compatible perceived VTS and VLS were included as variables. The results of the *t*-test (see Table 4.8) show that a statistically significant difference was obtained for 23 out of 33 variable pairs (i.e. in 70% of cases). The η^2 statistic (0.50) indicated a large effect size for 15 variables, a moderate effect size for five variables and a small effect size for three variables (Table 4.9). An exploration of the descriptive statistics revealed that the differences between mean scores were in opposite directions: the mean scores for perceived VTS were higher in 14 cases and the mean scores for individual VLS items were higher in 9 cases.

Discussion

The RQ1 reflects the main aim of this study, which was to explore the relationship between VTS and VLS used by elementary school learners of English as a FL. The results of the *t*-test showed that there was no statistically significant difference for 26 of 31 variables (84%). Three of the five variables where a statistically significant difference was found include two basic communication strategies[2] (*Using synonyms in conversations* and *Using circumlocution*). The results of the descriptive statistics suggest that learners whose teachers employ adequate teaching strategies (i.e. *Giving synonyms, Writing synonyms on board* and *Explain the meaning of a word in English*) use the two strategies more frequently than the learners whose teachers do not use these teaching strategies. These VLS are undoubtedly useful: not only do the learners acquire lexical items or expand their vocabulary by practising communicatively, but they also develop the skill of efficiently dealing with a potential communication breakdown due to lack of adequate linguistic knowledge

Table 4.8 Comparison of mean scores for perceived VTS and VLS (paired-samples *t*-test)

Variable		Mean values and standard deviations		*t*-test	*Sig.*
		Perceived VTS	*VLS use*		
perceivedVTS7-VLS1	n		358	− 3.000	0.003**
	Mean	1.6983	1.8296		
	δ	0.6807	0.6408		
perceivedVTS6-VLS1	n		358	10.156	0.000**
	Mean	2.2793	1.8296		
	δ	0.6569	0.6408		
perceivedVTS19-VLS1	n		357	− 1.366	0.173
	Mean	1.7731	1.8319		
	δ	0.6461	0.6402		
perceivedVTS9-VLS3	n		358	14.646	0.000**
	Mean	2.5112	1.8547		
	δ	0.6427	0.7030		
perceivedVTS3-VLS4	n		358	6.493	0.000**
	Mean	2.3352	2.0279		
	δ	0.6434	0.7095		

Table 4.8 (*Continued*)

Variable		Mean values and standard deviations		t-test	Sig.
		Perceived VTS	VLS use		
perceivedVTS7-VLS4	n		358	−6.380	0.000**
	Mean	1.6983	2.0279		
	δ	0.6807	0.7095		
perceivedVTS12-VLS4	n		358	−6.914	0.000**
	Mean	1.7235	2.0279		
	δ	0.5642	0.7095		
perceivedVTS16-VLS4	n		357	1.878	0.061
	Mean	2.1204	2.028		
	δ	0.6312	0.7105		
perceivedVTS29-VLS4	n		358	3.712	0.000**
	Mean	2.2263	2.0279		
	δ	0.6582	0.7095		
perceivedVTS8-VLS9	n		356	14.061	0.000**
	Mean	2.9298	2.4607		
	δ	0.2770	0.6062		

Table 4.8 (*Continued*)

Variable		Mean values and standard deviations		t-test	Sig.
		Perceived VTS	*VLS use*		
perceivedVTS13-VLS9	*n*		358	− 12.058	0.000**
	Mean	1.8659	2.4637		
	δ	0.8089	0.6058		
perceivedVTS15-VLS11	*n*		357	− 8.663	0.000**
	Mean	1.4622	1.8627		
	δ	0.6550	0.7077		
perceivedVTS10-VLS11	*n*		0.7061	− 1.293	0.197
	Mean	1.7978	1.8596		
	δ	0.6222	0.7061		
perceivedVTS11-VLS11	*n*		358	− 8.461	0.000**
	Mean	1.4972	1.8631		
	δ	0.6384	0.7067		
perceivedVTS24-VLS12	*n*		357	5.826	0.000**
	Mean	2.3725	2.1317		
	δ	0.6030	0.6927		

Table 4.8 (*Continued*)

Variable			Mean values and standard deviations		t-test	Sig.
			Perceived VTS	VLS use		
perceivedVTS20-VLS13		n	358	358	0.818	0.414
	Mean		1.2263	1.2011		
	δ		0.4984	0.4599		
perceivedVTS13-VLS14		n	358	358	0.709	0.479
	Mean		1.8659	1.8324		
	δ		0.8089	0.7521		
perceivedVTS18-VLS15		n	356	356	2.139	0.033*
	Mean		1.8034	1.7022		
	δ		0.6195	0.7129		
perceivedVTS8-VLS16		n	356	356	32.580	0.000**
	Mean		2.9298	1.6910		
	δ		0.2770	0.6457		
perceivedVTS13-VLS16		n	358	358	3.454	0.001**
	Mean		1.8659	1.6927		
	δ		0.8089	0.6443		

Table 4.8 (Continued)

Variable		Mean values and standard deviations		t-test	Sig.
		Perceived VTS	VLS use		
perceivedVTS17-VLS17	n		356	14.281	0.000**
	Mean	2.7528	2.1573		
	δ	0.4695	0.7105		
perceivedVTS17-VLS18	n		358	25.727	0.000**
	Mean	2.7542	1.7318		
	δ	0.4685	0.6132		
perceivedVTS26-VLS18	n		357	9.035	0.000**
	Mean	2.1204	1.7339		
	δ	0.6784	0.6129		
perceivedVTS25-VLS18	n		358	− 0.546	0.585
	Mean	1.7095	1.7318		
	δ	0.6648	0.6132		
perceivedVTS14-VLS19	n		357	1.931	0.054
	Mean	2.6415	2.5658		
	δ	0.4975	0.5942		

Table 4.8 (*Continued*)

Variable		Mean values and standard deviations		t-test	Sig.
		Perceived VTS	VLS use		
perceivedVTS29-VLS19	n		357	−7.640	0.000**
	Mean	2.2241	2.5658		
	δ	0.6579	0.5942		
perceivedVTS16-VLS19	n		356	−10.957	0.000**
	Mean	2.1180	2.5646		
	δ	0.6303	0.5946		
perceivedVTS2-VLS20	n		357	8.682	0.000**
	Mean	1.7003	1.3669		
	δ	0.6639	0.5780		
perceivedVTS4-VLS21	n		358	−8.347	0.000**
	Mean	1.7961	2.2291		
	δ	0.8029	0.7203		
perceivedVTS10-VLS25	n		355	−0.507	0.612
	Mean	1.7972	1.8197		
	δ	0.6230	0.6980		

Table 4.8 (*Continued*)

Variable		Mean values and standard deviations		t-test	Sig.
		Perceived VTS	VLS use		
perceivedVTS16-STRAT52	n		357	−1.708	0.088
	Mean	2.1204	2.2073		
	δ	0.6312	0.7873		
perceivedVTS29-STRAT52	n		358	0.367	0.714
	Mean	2.2263	2.2067		
	δ	0.6582	0.7863		
perceivedVTS22-VLS7	n		357	10.357	0.000**
	Mean	1.7759	1.3333		
	δ	0.7571	0.5692		

$*p < 0.05$
$**p < 0.01$

Table 4.9 Analysis of the size effect for the paired-samples *t*-test (perceived VTS and VLS)

Variable	η^2
perceivedVTS7-VLS1	0.01
perceivedVTS6-VLS1	0.22**
perceivedVTS9-VLS3	0.37**
perceivedVTS3-VLS4	0.10*
perceivedVTS7-VLS4	0.10*
perceivedVTS12-VLS4	0.11*
perceivedVTS29-VLS4	0.03
perceivedVTS8-VLS9	0.36**
perceivedVTS3-VLS9	0.29**
perceivedVTS5-VLS11	0.17**
perceivedVTS11-VLS11	0.17**
perceivedVTS24-VLS12	0.08*
perceivedVTS18-VLS15	0.01
perceivedVTS8-VLS16	0.75**
perceivedVTS13-VLS16	0.10*
perceivedVTS17-VLS17	0.36**
perceivedVTS17-VLS18	0.65**
perceivedVTS22-VLS18	0.19**
perceivedVTS25-VLS19	0.14**
perceivedVTS26-VLS19	0.25**
perceivedVTS2-VLS20	0.17**
perceivedVTS4-VLS21	0.16**
perceivedVTS22-VLS7	0.23**

**Large effect ($\eta^2 > 0.14$)
*Moderate effect ($\eta^2 > 0.06$)

or the inability to retrieve the desired lexical item. By using one of the above-mentioned communication strategies, learners not only retain the conversation, which boosts their self-confidence, but they also further develop their language skills and knowledge through an active use and exposure to the language input.

The next variable for which a statistically significant difference was determined was the VTS of *Presenting the meaning with a picture* related to the VLS of *Imaging the word's meaning*. This means that, if the teacher presents the meaning of a lexical item by using a picture illustrating its meaning, her learners will try to memorise it by linking it to the mental image of the word's meaning. This result is in line with the principle of visualisation in vocabulary learning and teaching (see Chapter 1). Visualisation, i.e. associating the meaning of lexical items with their mental image, aids the storing of lexical items in long-term memory, especially if the association is self-created. The possibility of learners developing this vocabulary learning strategy by being exposed to the adequate teaching strategy, which is suggested by the results of this study, has a clear practical teaching implication.

Furthermore, if teachers ask their learners to check the meaning of a word in a dictionary, learners will more often opt for this resource to learn new words. As the results of the descriptive statistics revealed that this VLS is rarely used by the learners involved in the study, and as the *t*-test results point to a potentially important role of the teacher in the development of the strategy, teachers should allocate some lesson time to training their learners in dictionary use. Thus, they can help develop the learners' awareness of the usefulness of dictionaries as (often the only) source of information on words. Needless to say, this VLS is one of the key strategies for independent learning of a *foreign* language.

Overall, our initial hypothesis was not supported by this study. Contrary to our expectations, the results indicated a weak association between VTS and VLS for this sample. These results imply that the learners' selection and use of VLS is independent of VTS. What follows is an examination of possible reasons that may explain the findings.

It is possible that learners at this age have an inventory of VLS that they have already acquired through observation or imitation (cf. Wenden, 2001). It is also possible that they have transferred learning strategies from other school subjects, as has been suggested by several previous studies (cf. Chamot, 1987; O'Malley *et al.*, 1985a). The learners in this sample, as mentioned before, have about 5 years' experience in formal learning. This conclusion can be corroborated by the results of the descriptive statistics according to which learners often or sometimes use almost all vocabulary learning strategies included in the questionnaire.

Furthermore, VLS develop parallel not only with learners' cognitive but also their linguistic development. This means that the use of some VLS presupposes an adequate level of linguistic knowledge *and* is dependent on linguistic characteristics of lexical items. It is possible that the learners in this sample have not yet reached the level of knowledge at which they could confidently use more elaborate VLS. This implies the existence of a natural progression in the development and use of learning strategies which has been suggested by Schmitt's study (1997). He, albeit with caution, concluded that the selection of VLS may be dependent on the learners' age, i.e. that not all VLS are equally adequate for all learners. Older learners may discard some strategies that they do not use any more and adopt new ones that are not popular with younger learners. The question of whether there is a natural progression in VLS development and what its characteristics might be should be investigated further. The results would be invaluable in planning and implementing VLS training tailored to learners' needs.

Also, a phenomenon – in many ways opposite to the one described above – a specific stagnation in the development of VLS may have occurred. It would imply that certain VLS become fossilised, i.e. learners do not continue to develop and expand their strategy inventories. This *fossilisation* of VLS might be caused by the learners' (often mistaken) impression as to the sufficient number, usefulness and efficiency of VLS they employ. It seems plausible to expect the fossilisation to be more noticeable with more successful learners: they think they are (strategically speaking) good learners because they achieve good results.

It is also possible that the weak link between teaching and learning strategies could be correlated to the role of the teachers. Two main reasons suggest themselves. First, teachers might lack understanding of factors influencing vocabulary acquisition and be unaware of VLS used by their learners. Consequently, they cannot adapt their teaching strategies to cater to the needs of the learners. Second, teachers might be using a limited selection of vocabulary teaching strategies failing to provide a variety of models of VLS for learners to imitate and internalise. Namely, the analysis of transcripts revealed that teachers select VTS according to their learners' age. For example, *Presenting words using word cards* is a VTS used by all three sixth-grade teachers, two seventh-grade teachers but not at all by eighth-grade teachers. Similarly, many other VTS involving a visual component (e.g. *Presenting a word by showing a picture, Drawing the word on the board, Match words with pictures, Using gestures in presenting words*, etc.) seem to be avoided by eighth-grade teachers. One of the reasons might be the fact that more abstract words, which cannot be presented by using pictures or gestures, are introduced at this level.

Moreover, very few VTS are used exclusively by 8th-grade teachers in the sample. One of them is the VTS *Guess meaning from context*, which again confirms the assumption that successful guessing presupposes a higher knowledge level. Generally, 8th-grade teachers used a smaller number of various VTS than the teachers in Grades 6 and 7. This is surprising, because one would expect that a higher level of cognitive development and linguistic knowledge of learners enables teachers to use a greater variety of VTS, which would cover complex lexical forms and relationships (cf. Chapter 1). The teachers' approach is not based on the textbooks they use, because the VTS in all learning materials analysed were varied and well balanced. Needless to say, in order to draw any general conclusions, one would have to conduct a study involving a larger sample of teachers.

As for the RQ2, i.e. the relationship between the learners' perception of VTS and their use of VLS, it seems that the frequency of VLS use does not depend on how learners perceive their teachers' VTS. Namely, the learners in the sample reported employing a number of VLS although they do not recognise compatible VTS used by their teacher (nine variables). But the learners also reported rarely using some VLS despite their belief that their teacher often uses compatible VTS (14 variables). In brief, no matter how often teachers seem to use a VTS (thus implicitly modelling a compatible VLS), learners independently decide when and how often they will employ their VLS.

Conclusion

The results of the present study lead to the conclusion that VLS used by learners in our sample are *independent* of VTS used by their teachers. Learners do, however, have an acquired inventory of VLS. The results may be taken as an indication that learning strategies are indeed one of the individual learner characteristics, i.e. an area where language learners may differ to a great extent.

Although statistically significant results have been obtained for five tested variables, the actual difference in the mean scores was very small. It is, therefore, questionable whether the difference obtained has any practical or theoretical significance.

The finding that the learners' VLS use is independent of perceived VTS raises an important question: can a teacher, by using a VTS, implicitly model the use of a compatible VLS? Obviously, using a VTS and giving a vocabulary task targeting the use of a particular VLS do not guarantee that learners will indeed use that VLS in doing the task. Learners may opt for VLS that are available to them or are more simple to use. In such situations, strategic goals set by teachers would not be accomplished, although the task would be successfully completed. This means that learners select their own VLS regardless of the VTS employed by their teachers. However, teachers must be aware of their learners' VLS in order to avoid their potential negative reactions to the teaching situations which may be caused by a mismatch between VTS and VLS preferred by learners. Learners, on the other hand, have to be aware of the usefulness, applicability and goals of a VTS in order to successfully 'copy' it onto their VLS. One must not forget that the learning and teaching results may be affected by the degree to which the goals set by the teacher and the learners' perception of the teaching situation coincide, or, as Kumaravadivelu (1991: 98) puts it: 'The narrower the gap between teacher intention and learner interpretation, the greater are the chances of achieving desired learning outcomes.'

The study's implications for teaching can be summed up as follows: training in vocabulary learning strategies should begin early enough for the learners to develop and acquire a satisfactory inventory of VLS. The training should preferably be explicit, as well as paced and adapted to the learners' age and the level of their cognitive and linguistic development. In order to be successful, strategy training demands a constant cooperation between teachers and learners in sharing their observations, experiences and problems connected with vocabulary learning.

Finally, a note of caution has to be sounded regarding a few limitations of the present study. First, we compared only compatible VL and teaching strategies, thus ignoring other possible interaction-effects and cross-reference. Second, the use of a questionnaire as the main instrument for measuring VLS has its disadvantages, such as the fact that a highly structured questionnaire (where all answers are offered) limits the learners' responses. Learners can also be unaware of their own learning strategies and therefore give random responses based on their impression and not real use of VLS. As a consequence, their true strategic profile might remain concealed. It is for this reason that researchers often opt for additional methods (e.g. think aloud protocols) to supplement the data.

Refraining from making unwarranted generalisations, we can only hope that efforts will be invested in future research that would try to shed some more light on patterns of interaction between vocabulary learning and teaching strategies.

Study 3: A Cross-linguistic Study of Vocabulary Learning Strategies Used by Elementary School Learners

Introduction

LLS, i.e. actions, behaviours, steps or techniques that learners use (often deliberately) to improve their progress in development of their language competence, have often been attributed an important role in the cognitive approach to L2 learning. The cognitive theory seems to suggest that LLS are general and universally applicable in various types of learning and similar learning situations. The advocates of the opposing view, however, see LLS as mostly domain-specific, i.e. linguistically oriented (cf. Kaplan, 1998) and disagree with an exclusive focus on psychological factors which overlooks the linguistic aspects involved in the process of L2 learning (see also Chapter 2).

The question that emerges from this criticism is: to what degree is the process of L2 learning characterised by general and to what degree by specific, linguistically oriented learning strategies? If the choice of LLS is influenced by the linguistic features of a language, learners of different foreign languages would opt for different LLS. Previous research on LLS has investigated the influence of various factors on the choice and use of LLS (see Chapter 3). The potential influence of social context on the choice of LLS (and learning success) has been recognised by a number of theoretical models of L2 acquisition (see Chapter 2). For example, in Abraham and Vann's (1987) L2 acquisition model LLS are influenced by environmental factors, i.e. the formal and informal learning context. Ellis's (1995) model sees LLS as having a mediating role between individual differences among learners and situational and social factors (target language, learning environment, task, gender) on one hand, and learning results on the other. This set of variables determines the learners' choice of LLS. The selected LLS influence the level and pace of language acquisition, or, vice versa, learning outcomes and the achieved language level can affect the selection of LLS. Moreover, Stern (1986) claims that, in addition to the social context, which is defined by sociolinguistic, sociocultural and socioeconomic factors, it is important to distinguish between second and FL learning context. In a L2 learning context, learners are exposed to a naturalistic language learning process. The distinction between second and FL is considered a significant variable by other researchers, too (cf. Hsiao & Oxford, 2002; LoCastro,

1994, 1995; Pearson, 1988). However, no studies explicitly dealt with the possible differences in LLS used by learners learning two different foreign languages in the same social context.

Aim

The aim of this study is to explore the differences in vocabulary learning strategies (VLS) used by learners of two different foreign languages. To this aim, data on VLS used by two groups of elementary school learners (learners of English and learners of German as a FL) have been collected and compared.

Methodology

Instruments

The data on VLS used by learners of English and learners of German were collected using the *VOLSQES* (Appendix B). *VOLSQES* is a 27-item questionnaire for measuring frequency of VLS use by elementary school learners. Each statement is followed by a Likert-type scale (1, never; 2, sometimes; 3, always). The reliability was 0.85 by Cronbach's alpha coefficients.

Participants

There were 675 participants in the study, including 322 learners of German and 353 learners of English as a FL. All participants attended elementary school and were aged between 11 and 14.

Procedure

The questionnaire was administered to all participants during their regular FL classes. After introducing the researcher, the teacher left the classroom. The researcher explained the aim of the study and gave detailed instructions on how to answer the questions. The survey lasted for 30 minutes on average.

The data were analysed by means of SPSS for Windows (Version 8.0). The main statistical procedure used was the independent samples *t*-test.

Results

In order to find out whether there are any differences in the use of VLS between learners of English and learners of German as a FL, we analysed the frequency distribution (using the Mean as an indicator of central tendency). The variable names were derived from the questionnaire statements with the variable number indicating the ordinal number of the statement in the questionnaire (e.g. VLS1 corresponds to the

Statement 1 in the questionnaire). The results of the descriptive analysis are shown in Table 4.10.

The order of the first eight most frequently used VLS indicates certain similarities in the use of VLS by the two groups of learners. These results are corroborated by the analysis of frequency distribution using the Mode as the indicator/criterion. First, the VLS most frequently used by both groups of learners are the following strategies: 9 (*Remembering words if they are written*), 19 (*Translating words into L1*) and 26 (*Testing oneself with word lists*). The learners of English use somewhat more often the following VLS: 5 (*Remembering words from films and TV programmes*), 10 (*Repeating new words aloud when studying*) and 22 (*Listening to songs in the target language*). In fact, VLS 22 seems to be one of the favourite VLS of learners of English, but rarely used by learners of German.

Second, both groups sometimes use the following VLS: 1 (Using new words in sentences), 2 (Making word lists), 3 (Regular reviewing outside classroom), 4 (Testing oneself), 9 (Using synonyms in conversations), 11 (Imaging the word's meaning), 12 (Associating new words with already known), 14 (Writing down words several times to remember them), 16 (Imaging the word's orthographical form), 17 (Using circumlocution), 18 (Associating words with the context), 21 (Repeating words mentally), 23 (Remembering words from books, magazines, etc.) and 24 (Using spaced word practice). Whereas the VLS 8 (Planning for vocabulary learning) and 27 (Remembering words from the Internet) are sometimes used by the learners of English, they are rarely used by learners of German. Contrary to this, VLS 15 (Reading and leafing through a dictionary) is sometimes used by learners of German and rarely by learners of English.

Finally, both groups rarely use the following VLS: 7 (Taking notes while reading for pleasure), 13 (Taking notes when watching films and TV programmes) and 20 (Grouping words together to study them).

In order to substantiate the results of the descriptive statistics, an independent-samples *t*-test was conducted to compare the VLS use scores for learners of English and learners of German. The null hypothesis put forward that there is no difference in the mean scores between the two groups of learners. The results of the *t*-test are shown in Table 4.11.

A total of 27 variables were tested. As can be seen in Table 4.11, 15 variables indicated a statistically significant difference. Therefore, the null hypothesis can be rejected, and the alternative hypothesis that there is a statistically significant difference between VLS used by learners of English and VLS used by learners of German can be accepted for the following variables:

Table 4.10 Frequency distributions of VLS for the two groups of learners (criterion: Mean)

	Learners of German (N = 327)				Learners of English (N = 358)		
	Variable	Mean (Mod)	δ		Variable	Mean (Mod)	δ
VLS19	Translating words into L1	2.6019 (3)	0.5826	VLS22	Listening to songs in the target language	2.6034 (3)	0.6771
VLS9	Remembering words if they are written down	2.5828 (3)	0.5527	VLS5	Remembering words from films and TV programmes	2.5726 (3)	0.6072
VLS26	Testing oneself with word lists	2.3436 (3)	0.7265	VLS19	Translating words into L1	2.5658 (3)	0.5942
VLS5	Remembering words from films and TV programmes	2.2324 (2)	0.7013	VLS9	Remembering words if they are written down	2.4637 (3)	0.6058
VLS10	Repeating new words aloud when studying	2.2178 (2)	0.7050	VLS6	Using synonyms in conversations	2.3128 (2)	0.6673
VLS12	Associating new words with already known	2.2043 (2)	0.6559	VLS10	Repeating new words aloud when studying	2.2514 (3)	0.7245
VLS6	Using synonyms in conversations	2.1896 (2)	0.7226	VLS21	Repeating words mentally	2.2291 (2)	0.7203
VLS21	Repeating words mentally	2.1442 (2)	0.7447	VLS26	Testing oneself with word lists	2.2067 (3)	0.7863
VLS4	Testing oneself	2.1407 (2)	0.6951	VLS23	Remembering words from books, magazines	2.2067 (2)	0.7270

Table 4.10 (Continued)

	Learners of German (N = 327)				*Learners of English (N = 358)*		
	Variable	*Mean (Mod)*	*δ*		*Variable*	*Mean (Mod)*	*δ*
VLS25	Connecting words to physical objects	2.1131 (2)	0.6756	VLS17	Using circumlocution	2.1573 (2)	0.7105
VLS2	Making word lists	2.0917 (2)	0.7896	VLS12	Associating new words with already known	2.1317 (2)	0.6927
VLS24	Using spaced word practice	2.0646	0.7236	VLS4	Testing oneself	2.0279	0.7095
VLS11	Imaging word's meaning	2.0277 (2)	0.7131	VLS2	Making word lists	2.0168 (2)	0.7848
VLS3	Regular reviewing outside classroom	1.9847 (2)	0.6249	VLS27	Remembering words from the Internet	1.9944 (2)	0.8084
VLS17	Using circumlocution	1.9231 (2)	0.7309	VLS11	Imaging word's meaning	1.8631 (2)	0.7067
VLS1	Using new words in sentences	1.8991 (2)	0.6159	VLS3	Regular reviewing outside classroom	1.8547 (2)	0.7030
VLS16	Imaging word's orthographical form	1.8405 (2)	0.7183	VLS24	Using spaced word practice	1.8403 (2)	0.7109
VLS23	Remembering words from books, magazines	1.8379 (2)	0.7272	VLS14	Writing down words repeatedly to remember them	1.8324 (2)	0.7521

Table 4.10 (Continued)

	Learners of German (N = 327)				Learners of English (N = 358)		
	Variable	Mean (Mod)	δ		Variable	Mean (Mod)	δ
VLS22	Listening to songs in the target language	1.8073 (1)	0.7611	VLS1	Using new words in sentences	1.8296 (2)	0.6408
VLS18	Associating words with the context	1.7415 (2)	0.6390	VLS25	Connecting words to physical objects	1.8179 (2)	0.6974
VLS15	Reading and leafing through dictionary	1.7399 (2)	0.7052	VLS8	Planning for vocabulary learning	1.7346 (2)	0.7097
VLS14	Writing down words repeatedly to remember them	1.7301 (2)	0.6978	VLS18	Associating words with the context	1.7318 (2)	0.6132
VLS8	Planning for vocabulary learning	1.7239 (1)	0.7383	VLS15	Reading and leafing through dictionary	1.7031 (1)	0.7121
VLS20	Grouping words together to study them	1.6431 (1)	0.6996	VLS16	Imaging word's orthographical form	1.6927 (2)	0.6443
VLS27	Remembering words from the Internet	1.6411 (1)	0.7254	VLS20	Grouping words together to study them	1.3669 (1)	0.5780
VLS7	Taking notes while reading for pleasure	1.3242 (1)	0.5638	VLS7	Taking notes while reading for pleasure	1.3333 (1)	0.5692

Table 4.10 (*Continued*)

	Learners of German (N =327)				*Learners of English (N =358)*		
	Variable	*Mean (Mod)*	*δ*		*Variable*	*Mean (Mod)*	*δ*
VLS13	Taking notes when watching films and TV programmes	1.1595 (1)	0.4357	VLS13	Taking notes when watching films and TV programmes	1.2011 (1)	0.4599

Table 4.11 Comparison of mean scores for learners of English and learners of German (*t*-test)

Variable	Mean		*t-test*	*Sig.*
	German	*English*		
VLS1 Using new words in sentences	1.8991	1.8296	− 1.446	0.149
VLS2 Making word lists	2.0917	2.0168	− 1.245	0.213
VLS3 Regular reviewing outside classroom	1.9847	1.8547	− 2.558	0.011*
VLS4 Testing oneself	2.1407	2.0279	− 2.097	0.036*
VLS5 Remembering words from films and TV programmes	2.2324	2.5726	6.759	0.000**
VLS6 Using synonyms in conversations	2.1896	2.3128	2.321	0.021*
VLS7 Taking notes while reading for pleasure	1.3242	1.3333	0.212	0.833
VLS8 Planning for vocabulary learning	1.7239	1.7346	0.193	0.847
VLS9 Remembering words if they are written down	2.5828	2.4637	− 2.690	0.007*
VLS10 Repeating new words aloud when studying	2.2178	2.2514	0.614	0.540
VLS11 Imaging the word's meaning	2.0277	1.8631	− 3.026	0.003**
VLS12 Associating new words with already known	2.2043	2.1317	− 1.401	0.162
VLS13 Taking notes when watching films and TV programmes	1.1595	1.2011	0.244	0.807
VLS14 Writing down words repeatedly to remember them	1.7301	1.8324	1.839	0.066
VLS15 Reading and leafing through dictionary	1.7399	1.7031	− 0.677	0.499

Table 4.11 (*Continued*)

Variable	Mean		t-test	Sig.
	German	English		
VLS16 Imaging the word's orthographical form	1.8405	1.6927	−2.836	0.005**
VLS17 Using circumlocution	1.9231	2.1573	4.239	0.000**
VLS18 Associating words with the context	1.7415	1.7318	−0.202	0.840
VLS19 Translating words into L1	2.6019	2.5658	−0.797	0.425
VLS20 Grouping words together to study them	1.6431	1.3669	−5.588	0.000**
VLS21 Repeating words mentally	2.1442	2.2291	1.515	0.130
VLS22 Listening to songs in the target language	1.8073	2.6034	14.408	0.000**
VLS23 Remembering words from books, magazines	1.8379	2.2067	6.630	0.000**
VLS24 Using spaced word practice	2.0646	1.8403	−4.080	0.000**
VLS25 Connecting words to physical objects	2.1131	1.8179	−5.613	0.000**
VLS26 Testing oneself with word lists	2.3436	2.2067	−2.357	0.019*
VLS27 Remembering words from the Internet	1.6411	1.9944	5.986	0.000**

*$p < 0.05$
**$p < 0.01$

VLS3 Regular reviewing outside classroom
VLS4 Testing oneself
VLS5 Remembering words from films and TV programmes
VLS6 Using synonyms in conversations
VLS9 Remembering words if they are written down
VLS11 Imaging the word's meaning
VLS16 Imaging the word's orthographical form
VLS17 Using circumlocution
VLS20 Grouping words together to study them
VLS22 Listening to songs in the target language
VLS23 Remembering words from books, magazines etc.
VLS24 Using spaced word practice
VLS25 Connecting words to physical objects
VLS26 Testing oneself with word lists
VLS27 Remembering words from the Internet

As for the other variables, there was no statistically significant difference. Therefore, the null hypothesis that there is no difference in the use of VLS between learners of English and learners of German can be accepted.

An inspection of the descriptive statistics revealed that in nine cases the Mean score for learners of German was significantly higher that that of learners of English. According to the classification proposed earlier (see Study 1), five variables, i.e. VLS, are strategies of formal practising (VLS3 *Regular reviewing outside classroom*, VLS4 *Testing oneself*, VLS9 *Remembering words if they are written down*, VLS24 *Using spaced word practice*, VLS26 *Testing oneself with word lists*), and the other four VLS belong to the group of strategies for self-initiated independent vocabulary learning (VLS11 *Imaging the word's meaning*, VLS16 *Imaging the word's orthographical form*, VLS20 *Grouping words together to study them*, VLS25 *Connecting words to physical objects*). Learners of English, according to the descriptive statistics, use the following six VLS significantly more often than learners of German: VLS5 *Remembering words from films and TV programmes*, VLS22 *Listening to songs in the target language*, VLS23 *Remembering words from books, magazines, etc.*, VLS27 *Remembering words from the Internet*, VLS6 *Using synonyms in conversations*, VLS17 *Using circumlocution*. All six VLS belong to the group of VLS used in self-initiated vocabulary learning.

Discussion and conclusions

The results of the study lead to the following conclusions.

There is a set of VLS that can be considered core VLS and that are applicable in various learning contexts (e.g. *Translating words into L1, Testing oneself using word lists with translation, Remembering words if they are written down*, etc.). As they do not seem to be influenced by external factors (learning context, social context, language policy of a country, etc.), they are universal and can be employed when learning any FL.

Learners of German in this sample seem to approach language learning in a traditional way which is characteristic of school-based formal language instruction. This includes the use of memory strategies and the metacognitive aspect of planned learning. The English learners' approach to vocabulary learning is more spontaneous and indirect thus possibly creating opportunities for incidental vocabulary acquisition.

The major difference observed between the two groups of learners can be attributed to the degree to which the learners are exposed to the target language. Learners of English seem to benefit from the fact that films and other TV programmes in Croatia are subtitled and not dubbed. They are exposed practically daily to authentic English. Because of a large amount of the language input, learning of English has certain characteristics of L2 learning environment. In such a learning context, learners have an opportunity to develop VLS uncommon in formal learning contexts (cf. Lamb, 2004).

No conclusions could be made related to the direct influence of the target language on the selection of VLS. The assumption that linguistic features of a language affect the use of VLS can to a degree be supported by only one VLS (VLS14 *Writing down words several times*), which is less frequently used by learners of German. This issue, however, has to be further investigated.

To sum up, the results of the study did not reveal any differences in the use of VLS between learners of English and learners of German that can be attributed to the linguistic features of lexical items. However, the results imply that the position of the FL in the learning context does affect the selection and use of the VLS. The step that future research may take is a cross-linguistic study covering other foreign languages in order to further explore potential similarities and differences in the strategic approach to vocabulary learning.

Notes

1. In Croatia, elementary education lasts for eight years (Grades 1–8) from ages 7 to 15.
2. See Chapter 2 for the discussion of distinction between communication and learning strategies. As communication strategies are considered to have the

capacity of positively influencing the language learning process because they potentially expose the learner to functional practicing and additional language input (*cf.* Williams & Burden, 2001), it was decided to include them in the study.

Chapter 5

Summary: Some Implications for Practice and Research, and Conclusions

Over the last three decades there has been growing interest in research on language learning strategies as a result of the efforts made by language educators to understand better the ways in which individual learners approach second and foreign language learning and what effects their approaches may have on the acquisition process and, ultimately, on achievement. The main goal of this research orientation is to enhance the role of the individual learner in the language learning process. In this book we have focused on exploring the specific subset of language learning strategies, namely that of vocabulary learning strategies, which are assumed to be an important aspect of second language vocabulary acquisition.

In this concluding chapter we will first review the topics and issues discussed in the foregoing chapters and then address the implications for practice. Finally, we will foreshadow the paths that future research may take.

Summary and Conclusions

The first three chapters presented the theoretical background and research review. The first chapter started by analysing factors affecting second language vocabulary learning and acquisition. Although language learning strategies were primarily viewed from the cognitive angle, the fact that the cognitive approach to language learning is reputed to neglect the role of linguistic factors in second language acquisition was not overlooked. Therefore, starting from the assumption that language learning strategies are not the only determinant in vocabulary learning and acquisition, a number of other aspects were considered, such as the role of L1, the learning context, inherent linguistic features of lexical items, etc. The chapter then went on to discuss the issue of the mental lexicon, i.e. its development and organisation in general as well as the similarities and differences between L1 lexicon and

L2 lexicon. With regard to L2 lexicon, relevant research findings suggested that the organisation of the mental lexicon and vocabulary development are in a causal and dynamic relationship with each other, and that vocabulary learning strategies may significantly contribute to determining the quality of that relationship. The last portion of the chapter summarised vocabulary teaching strategies on the basis of literature inspection. The rationale for this was to give a structured overview of numerous vocabulary teaching strategies, to emphasise the importance of controlled explicit vocabulary instruction, and to recognise the indisputably important role of the teacher and teaching strategies in formal L2 instruction.

The subsequent chapter began with the discussion of the role of learning strategies in the cognitive theory and other relevant theories and language learning models. It was argued that, in order to understand the impact of the cognitive theory on second language acquisition, the interaction between language and cognition needs to be determined (cf. Ellis, 2000; Skehan, 2000). Next, the approaches to defining and describing features of language learning strategies were reviewed. Interestingly, in spite of the fact that scholars have failed to come to a consensus concerning the definition of learning strategies, most of them do not seem to question the significance of learning strategies in second language acquisition. On the basis of existing definitions, a summative definition was proposed and features of learning strategies listed.

The third chapter first looked at previous research related to vocabulary learning strategies. It evaluated research studies addressing the significance of various factors that proved relevant in the selection of vocabulary learning strategies. This included variables such as gender, age, motivation, personality traits, proficiency level, the nature of the language task, etc. The chapter went on to discuss the potentials of vocabulary learning strategy training. The key postulation is the following: if language learning strategies are amenable to change, then, by modifying the learners' strategic behaviours, we can wield influence on the quality of second language learning and, ultimately, on attainment. The fact that research on the interaction between strategy training and strategy acquisition is still inconclusive calls for a change in the approach to both research and strategy instruction. Rather than focusing on measuring the effect of training single or a few individual vocabulary learning strategies, research should take an 'all-inclusive' turn if it is to justify the significance of vocabulary learning strategies in vocabulary acquisition. Naturally, strategy training should follow suit. Otherwise, the above-mentioned postulation would remain a mere speculation. This chapter concluded with a critical review of research methods and instruments for strategy assessment. We outlined the advantages and pitfalls of each research method and, more to the point, argued in favour of triangulation.

In the fourth chapter, three studies on vocabulary learning strategies were described in detail.

The first study focused on the development of an instrument for measuring vocabulary learning strategies used by primary school learners. The study, involving several factor analyses, resulted with *Vocabulary Learning Strategy Questionnaire for Elementary Schools* (VOLSQES), which is not only valid and reliable, but is also adapted to the variable to be measured as well as to the population targeted by the research.

The second study was spurred by one of the burning issues often raised in the field of second language acquisition research, namely, whether and in what way instruction affects the development, acquisition and use of language learning strategies. Nevertheless, prior to the study described in the previous chapter, no empirical research on the relationship between teaching and learning strategies had been undertaken. Our study set out to investigate whether foreign language learners' use of vocabulary learning strategies can be related to the vocabulary teaching strategies employed by their teachers. Contrary to our expectations, the results indicated a weak association between vocabulary teaching strategies and vocabulary learning strategies. In spite of the fact that a few variables reached statistical significance, their practical significance is questionable. The results of the study lead to several conclusions. First, the learners' use of vocabulary learning strategies is independent of vocabulary teaching strategies employed by their teachers. Moreover, there seems to be no relationship between the use of vocabulary learning strategies and learners' perception of vocabulary teaching strategies. Learners do have an inventory of strategies which they employ in dealing with vocabulary learning tasks that they might have adopted earlier or transferred from other learning situations, i.e. school subjects. The training of vocabulary learning strategies seems predominantly implicit and sporadic, and based on the teachers' assessment, interest, knowledge, experience and intuition.

The results of the cross-linguistic study of vocabulary learning strategies (Study 3) suggest that the selection of vocabulary learning strategies may be governed by the foreign language being learnt, i.e. by its position in the wider social context. Apart from a few vocabulary learning strategies used by both groups of learners involved in the study, which may be considered core vocabulary learning strategies, learners of different foreign languages will use different vocabulary learning strategies. Further research is necessary to investigate the question whether the notion of core vocabulary learning strategies can be substantiated, i.e. whether it would be possible to single out vocabulary learning strategies that are applicable in a variety of vocabulary learning situations and that are acceptable to the majority of foreign language learners. It is this set of vocabulary learning strategies whose training would be worthwhile and would be the initial stage of any vocabulary learning strategy training. Later steps in strategy training could then focus on elaborating and expanding the basic inventory of vocabulary learning strategies in line with the learners' cognitive, affective and linguistic development.

Implications for Practice and Future Research

The findings of the studies reported in the previous chapter suggest interventions in several pedagogical areas be made: foreign language instruction, teacher education and design of teaching and learning materials. In their work, teachers intuitively allude to VLS, but such an implicit approach to VLS training does not seem to be fruitful enough in terms of their effect on learners' selection and application of VLS. Mere imitation of the teachers' VTS and their copying onto one's own VLS does not seem to lead to further development of VLS. Therefore, explicit vocabulary learning strategy training imposes itself as a necessity. Explicit vocabulary learning strategy training involves, as a rule, raising the learners' awareness of their own strategies, introducing them to new ones, and giving them any opportunity to apply, analyse and adopt new vocabulary learning strategies. Learners also have to be familiar with the aims of vocabulary learning strategy training, that is understand the usefulness and applicability of individual VLS, as well as the long-term value of an extensive repertoire of VLS. A broad inventory of VLS is one of the features of an autonomous learner.

Learning materials should have an extremely important role in VLS training. As research results suggest, teachers often rely on the materials they teach from. Therefore, learning materials should include activities for explicit and implicit work on VLS development. Similarly, teachers' books should contain adequate guidelines on how to approach VLS training. Furthermore, the materials should suggest a variety of VTS which are more closely linked to VLS, i.e. VTS that are directed towards development and use of VLS through different tasks, such as awareness raising tasks, tasks integrating strategic and linguistic goals, and tasks aiming at active use and constant recycling of VLS in different contexts. Such training tasks aim at stimulating learners and providing them with opportunities to think about and evaluate their own use of VLS. Obviously, the tasks should be adapted to the learners' age and level, as well as their interests and needs.

VLS training ought to commence early enough in order for learners to develop and acquire a wide repertoire of VLS. The order of training of individual strategies has to concur with the learners' cognitive and linguistic development.

A precondition of a successful VLS training is an informed teacher. First of all, teachers need to understand the difference between vocabulary teaching and learning strategies. They should acquire basic knowledge of learning strategies in their pre-service training courses and expand it through in-service seminars and workshops on integrating strategy training into language courses. Moreover, teachers should have knowledge of their learners' strategic profiles in order to effectively adapt their teaching strategies and to help learners to reflect on their own learning. To this aim, a questionnaire, such as VOLSQES, can be an efficient screening instrument providing useful information for both teacher and for learners. Simultaneously, this questionnaire can be used as a training tool: by filling it in, learners become aware of their own strategies but also discover new ones.[1] By integrating VLS training with concrete vocabulary learning tasks teachers provide their learners with an opportunity to immediately test and evaluate the new VLS. In summary, an efficient development and employment of VLS requires a persistent cooperation between learners and teachers who have to inform each other, share experiences and knowledge, analyse problems and suggest solutions. Teachers and learners have to share the responsibility that the process of learning and teaching entails in order to meet the aims of foreign language instruction in primary schools, which is the development of basic communicative competence and ability for lifelong foreign language learning.

The overarching conclusion emanating from the studies reported on is that vocabulary learning strategies are highly idiosyncratic and need to be regarded accordingly. This conclusion may have numerous implications both for further research and teaching practice. If vocabulary learning strategies are in effect idiosyncratic, then a standardised questionnaire (or any other standardised data collection method for that matter) is not universally applicable in research, because it alone cannot fully grasp all strategic characteristics of a particular sample. This assumption justifies designing a special questionnaire tailored to the research context and using other methods such as retrospective interviews or think-aloud protocols to complement the data.

As for future research, the earlier described questions that emerged from the studies and need to be addressed are manifold. We suggest only a few directions that future research may follow:

- Do learners' personality traits affect the relationship between VLS and VTS? As previous research suggested that a number of factors affect the use of learning strategies (e.g. gender, proficiency level, achievement, etc.), it seems safe to assume that taking these variables into consideration would affect the research results.
- Do learning strategies develop parallel with cognitive and linguistic development, is the choice of learning strategies influenced by the degree of cognitive and linguistic development or are learning strategies affected by the phenomenon that can be referred to as fossilisation of learning strategies? Without a longitudinal research design we cannot begin to answer this question.
- Does the process of evaluation, i.e. approach to assessment and testing of vocabulary knowledge, influence the selection and development of VLS?

Continuous and unrelenting research on vocabulary learning strategies is what we recommend and what we hope for, because it is the only possible path to gaining better insight into the complex processes of vocabulary learning and teaching and, ultimately, into foreign language lexical development.

Note

1. If a questionnaire is to be used as a training instrument then the pilot version (Appendix A) can be recommended as a more comprehensive inventory of VLS suitable to various levels and ages of learners.

Appendix A

BACKGROUND QUESTIONNAIRE

Please complete this part of the questionnaire first.

(1) Gender (circle): m – f
(2) Grade_____
(3) School_____
(4) What was your half-term grade in the foreign language you are learning?_____
(5) How long have you been learning this foreign language?_____
_____

(6) If you have cable or satellite TV with programmes in the foreign language you are learning at school answer the following questions:
  a. How often do you watch programmes in the foreign language you are learning at school?_____
  b. What programmes do you usually watch?_____
_____

Foreign languages can be learnt in various ways. The aim of this questionnaire is to find out how YOU learn foreign language words. Please answer how you really learn and not how you think you should learn or how somebody else learns.

For each statement you can choose one of the following responses:

1-never   2-sometimes   3 – always

Circle the response that best describes how you learn. There are no right or wrong answers to these statements.

1.*	I use new words in a sentence in order to remember them.	1	2	3
2.*	I make word lists and write their translations in my mother tongue.	1	2	3
3.*	I review words regularly outside the classroom.	1	2	3
4.*	I test myself to check if I remember the words.	1	2	3
5.*	I pick up words from films and TV programmes I watch.	1	2	3
6.*	I use familiar words in various ways in new situations in order to remember them.	1	2	3
7.*	I ask the teacher to explain the meaning of the word.	1	2	3
8.*	I remember a word by remembering its location in the notebook, textbook, or on the board.	1	2	3
9.*	If I cannot remember a word in conversations, I use another one with a similar meaning.	1	2	3
10.*	I use rhyme in order to remember a word.	1	2	3
11.	I remember a word by remembering its initial letter.	1	2	3
12.*	If I do not understand a word, I look it up in a bilingual dictionary.	1	2	3
13.	I remember words that are in some way similar.	1	2	3
14.*	If I hear a new word in class, I immediately write it down.	1	2	3
15.	I like to be corrected if I misuse a word.	1	2	3
16.	I analyse word parts in order to guess the meaning of a word.	1	2	3
17.*	I write down words while I read books and magazines for pleasure.	1	2	3
18.*	I make word cards.	1	2	3
19.*	I look for similarities in sound and meaning between words in my mother tongue and foreign words (cognates) in order to guess the meaning.	1	2	3
20.*	I plan for vocabulary learning in advance.	1	2	3

21.*	I remember a word if I see it written down.	1	2	3
22.*	I try to use a word in a sentence correctly.	1	2	3
23.*	I say a word out loud repeatedly in order to remember it.	1	2	3
24.*	I connect an image with a word's meaning in order to remember it.	1	2	3
25.	If I do not understand a word, I look it up in a monolingual dictionary.	1	2	3
26.	If I cannot remember a word in conversations, I use gestures.	1	2	3
27.*	I associate new words with the ones I already know.	1	2	3
28.	I tape record the words and then listen to the tape.	1	2	3
29.*	I write down words when I watch films and TV programmes.	1	2	3
30.*	If I do not understand a word, I ask for help.	1	2	3
31.*	I write down words repeatedly to remember them.	1	2	3
32.*	I read and leaf through a dictionary to learn some new words.	1	2	3
33.*	I remember 'complicated' words because they stand out.	1	2	3
34.*	I make a mental picture of a word's written form in order to remember it.	1	2	3
35.*	If I cannot remember a word in a conversation, I describe it in my own words in the foreign language.	1	2	3
36.*	I imagine a context in which a word could be used in order to remember it.	1	2	3
37.*	I translate the words into my mother tongue to understand them.	1	2	3
38.	I use colours and highlighters to mark new words in a text.	1	2	3
39.*	I group words together in order to remember them.	1	2	3
40.	If I cannot remember a word in the foreign language, I make one up.	1	2	3
41.*	I remember a word if I encounter it many times.	1	2	3

42.*	I 'act out' the meaning of a new word to remember it.	1	2	3
43.*	I try to use the new words I learn immediately in conversations or writing.	1	2	3
44.*	I repeat the word mentally in order to remember it.	1	2	3
45.*	I try to guess the meaning of a new word from the context.	1	2	3
46.*	I remember a word if I associate it with pictures, drawings or illustrations.	1	2	3
47.*	I listen to songs in the foreign language and try to understand the words.	1	2	3
48.*	I pick up words while reading books and magazines in the foreign language.	1	2	3
49.*	I use spaced word practice in order to remember words.	1	2	3
50.*	When I test myself I try to give the word's definition in the foreign language.	1	2	3
51.	If I cannot remember a word in conversations, I use a word in my mother tongue.	1	2	3
52.*	I remember a word if I remember the context in which I heard it.	1	2	3
53.	I connect new words with words in another foreign language to remember them.	1	2	3
54.*	I pick up words from computer games.	1	2	3
55.*	If I cannot remember a word in conversations, I ask for help.	1	2	3
56.*	I remember a word if I connect it with my personal experience.	1	2	3
57.*	I connect words with other words with similar or opposite meanings.	1	2	3
58.*	I connect words to physical objects to remember them	1	2	3
59.*	I ask somebody to test me on words (e.g. parent, sibling, friend).	1	2	3
60.	If I cannot remember a word in conversations, I don't say anything.	1	2	3

61.*	I remember a word if I like it.	1	2	3
62.	If I encounter an unknown word, I ignore it if I understand what the text is about.	1	2	3
63.	I look up words in computer dictionaries.	1	2	3
64.*	I practice with friends in order to remember words.	1	2	3
65.*	I keep a separate vocabulary notebook.	1	2	3
66.	If I do not know a word, I look it up in the textbook glossary.	1	2	3
67.*	I test myself with word lists to check if I remember the words.	1	2	3
68.	I review words only before a test.	1	2	3
69.*	I pick up words from the Internet.	1	2	3

NB: Statements marked with * formed the reduced 53-item version of the questionnaire used in the main study of Study 1.

Appendix B

Vocabulary Learning Strategy Questionnaire
for Elementary Schools

Foreign languages can be learnt in various ways. The aim of this questionnaire is to find out how YOU learn foreign language words. Please answer how you really learn and not how you think you should learn or how somebody else learns.

For each statement you can choose one of the following responses:

1-never   2-sometimes   3-always

Circle the response that best describes how you learn. There are no right or wrong answers to these statements.

1.	I use new words in a sentence in order to remember them.	1	2	3
2.	I make word lists and write their translations in my mother tongue.	1	2	3
3.	I review words regularly outside the classroom.	1	2	3
4.	I test myself to check if I remember the words.	1	2	3
5.	I pick up words from films and TV programmes I watch.	1	2	3
6.	If I cannot remember a word in a conversation, I use another one with a similar meaning.	1	2	3
7.	I write down words while I read books and magazines for pleasure.	1	2	3
8.	I plan for vocabulary learning in advance.	1	2	3
9.	I remember a word if I see it written down.	1	2	3
10.	I say a word out loud repeatedly in order to remember it.	1	2	3

11.	I connect an image with a word's meaning in order to remember it.	1	2	3
12.	I associate new words with the ones I already know.	1	2	3
13.	I write down words when I watch films and TV programmes.	1	2	3
14.	I write down words repeatedly to remember them.	1	2	3
15.	I read and leaf through a dictionary to learn some new words.	1	2	3
16.	I make a mental image a word's written form in order to remember it.	1	2	3
17.	If I cannot remember a word in a conversation, I describe it in my own words in the foreign language.	1	2	3
18.	I imagine a context in which a word could be used in order to remember it.	1	2	3
19.	I translate the words into my mother tongue to understand them.	1	2	3
20.	I group words together in order to remember them.	1	2	3
21.	I repeat the word mentally in order to remember it.	1	2	3
22.	I listen to songs in the foreign language and try to understand the words.	1	2	3
23.	I pick up words while reading books and magazines in the foreign language.	1	2	3
24.	I use spaced word practice in order to remember words.	1	2	3
25.	I connect words to physical objects to remember them	1	2	3
26.	I test myself with word lists to check if I remember the words.	1	2	3
27.	I pick up words from the Internet.	1	2	3

Supplement

The aim of this part of the questionnaire is to find out what vocabulary work you do <u>in class</u>, i.e. what <u>your teacher</u> does.

For each statement you can choose one of the following responses:

1-never   2-sometimes   3-always

Circle the response that best describes what your teacher does. <u>There are no right or wrong answers to these statements.</u>

1.	The teacher helps us to remember words by giving us the initial letter of the word.	1	2	3
2.	The teacher tells us to group words.	1	2	3
3.	The teacher gives us (oral and written) tests to check our vocabulary knowledge.	1	2	3
4.	The teacher tells us to mentally repeat words in order to remember them.	1	2	3
5.	The teacher gives us instructions and advice on how to study words at home.	1	2	3
6.	The teacher gives several example sentences in which new words are used.	1	2	3
7.	In tests, the teacher gives us a word and we have to use it in a sentence.	1	2	3
8.	The teacher writes new words on the board.	1	2	3
9.	The teacher asks us to review words regularly at home.	1	2	3
10.	The teacher uses real objects when explaining the meaning of new words.	1	2	3
11.	The teacher tells us to make a mental picture of the new word's meaning in order to remember it	1	2	3
12.	When testing, the teacher shows a picture and we have to supply the word in the foreign language.	1	2	3
13.	The teacher tells us to write down the word several times to remember it.	1	2	3
14.	The teacher asks for translation into the mother tongue.	1	2	3
15.	The teacher draws the word's meaning on the board.	1	2	3
16.	When testing, the teacher gives us a word in the mother tongue and we have to translate it into the foreign language.	1	2	3

17.	The teacher explains the new word's meaning in the foreign language.	1	2	3
18.	The teacher asks us to look up the new word in the dictionary.	1	2	3
19.	The teacher tells us to use the new word in a sentence.	1	2	3
20.	The teacher advises us to write down words we hear in films and TV programmes in the foreign language.	1	2	3
21.	When we cannot remember a word, the teacher reminds us of where it appears in the textbook.	1	2	3
22.	The teacher advises us to write down words when we read books and magazines for pleasure in the foreign language.	1	2	3
23.	The teacher points to the similarities in sound and meaning between mother tongue and foreign language words (cognates).	1	2	3
24.	The teacher connects new words with the ones we have learnt previously.	1	2	3
25.	The teacher tells us to imagine a situation in which the new word would be used in order to remember it.	1	2	3
26.	The teacher describes a situation in which the new word could be used.	1	2	3
27.	The teacher tells us to underline new words in the text.	1	2	3
28.	The words we learn are repeatedly mentioned in foreign language classes.	1	2	3
29.	When testing, the teacher gives the foreign language word and we have to translate it into our mother tongue.	1	2	3

Please complete this part of the questionnaire too.

(1) Gender (circle): m – f
(2) Grade_____
(3) School_____
(4) How long has your current foreign language teacher been teaching you? _____
(5) Your final grade in the foreign language_____
(6) How old were you when you started learning the foreign language?
_____

Appendix C

Results of the Factor Analyses
(pilot study)

Table C.1: Initial statistics for pVLS (69 items)

Component	Total	%Variance	Cumulative%
1	7.751	11.233	11.233
2	4.233	6.134	17.368
3	3.444	4.991	22.359
4	2.935	4.254	26.612
5	2.692	3.902	30.514
6	2.372	3.438	33.951
7	2.251	3.262	37.213
8	2.196	3.182	40.395
9	2.166	3.139	43.534
10	1.914	2.774	46.308
11	1.842	2.670	48.977
12	1.809	2.621	51.599
13	1.733	2.512	54.111
14	1.659	2.405	56.516
15	1.642	2.379	58.895
16	1.475	2.138	61.033
17	1.383	2.005	63.038
18	1.298	1.881	64.919

Table C.1 (*Continued*)

19	1.272	1.844	66.763
20	1.200	1.740	68.503
21	1.187	1.721	70.224
22	1.130	1.638	71.861
23	1.065	1.544	73.405
24	1.047	1.518	74.923
25	0.992	1.437	76.360
26	0.977	1.416	77.776
27	0.908	1.316	79.092
28	0.857	1.242	80.334
29	0.834	1.209	81.543
30	0.798	1.156	82.698
31	0.785	1.138	83.836
32	0.733	1.062	84.898
33	0.712	1.031	85.929
34	0.671	0.973	86.902
35	0.633	0.917	87.819
36	0.621	0.900	88.719
37	0.558	0.809	89.528
38	0.526	0.762	90.290
39	0.499	0.724	91.014
40	0.482	0.699	91.713
41	0.451	0.654	92.366
42	0.429	0.621	92.988
43	0.395	0.573	93.561
44	0.385	0.559	94.120
45	0.362	0.524	94.644

Table C.1 (*Continued*)

46	0.344	0.498	95.142
47	0.327	0.474	95.616
48	0.307	0.445	96.061
49	0.272	0.395	96.456
50	0.255	0.370	96.825
51	0.247	0.358	97.183
52	0.221	0.320	97.503
53	0.192	0.278	97.780
54	0.186	0.270	98.050
55	0.161	0.234	98.284
56	0.148	0.215	98.498
57	0.130	0.189	98.687
58	0.127	0.184	98.871
59	0.119	0.172	99.043
60	0.110	0.160	99.203
61	9.608×10^{-2}	0.139	99.342
62	8.052×10^{-2}	0.117	99.459
63	7.924×10^{-2}	0.115	99.573
64	6.832×10^{-2}	9.901×10^{-2}	99.672
65	6.292×10^{-2}	9.119×10^{-2}	99.764
66	5.316×10^{-2}	7.704×10^{-2}	99.841
67	4.584×10^{-2}	6.643×10^{-2}	99.907
68	3.706×10^{-2}	5.370×10^{-2}	99.961
69	2.704×10^{-2}	3.919×10^{-2}	100.000

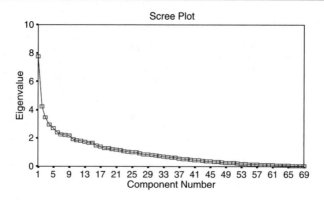

Figure C.1: Scree plot (initial 69 pVLS variables)

Table C.2: Varimax rotation of three-factor solution for pVLS items

Variable		*Components*			h²
		1	*2*	*3*	
pVLS5	Remembering words from films and TV programmes	0.614			0.788
pVLS41	Multiple encounters with a word	0.588		0.325	0.746
pVLS61	Affective associations	0.538			0.722
pVLS33	Remembering 'complicated' words	0.524			0.735
pVLS35	Using circumlocution	0.502			0.713
pVLS48	Remembering words from books, magazines, etc0.	0.491			0.754
pVLS6	Using known words in new contexts	0.464	0.333		0.599

Table C.2 (*Continued*)

pVLS43	Using new words in speaking or writing	0.427		0.305	0.698
pVLS69	Remembering words from the Internet	0.400			0.740
pVLS54	Remembering words from computer games	0.391		− 0.387	0.830
pVLS22	Accurate usage of words in sentences	0.388			0.765
pVLS47	Listening to songs in the foreign language	0.388			0.758
pVLS36	Imaging the context in which a word would be used	0.388	0.302		0.662
pVLS56	Associating words with personal experience	0.375			0.637
pVLS27	Associating new words with already known	0.365	0.338		0.786
pVLS9	Using synonyms in conversations to make up for lack of knowledge	0.340			0.760
pVLS17	Noting down words while reading for pleasure	0.326			0.800
pVLS60	Abandoning message	− 0.304			0.717
pVLS24	Imaging word's meaning	0.328	0.643		0.776

Table C.2 (*Continued*)

pVLS58	Connecting words with physical objects		0.563		0.652
pVLS34	Imaging word's orthographical form	0.369	0.529		0.800
pVLS45	Guessing from context		0.516		0.713
pVLS1	Using new words in sentences		0.480		0.717
pVLS42	Use physical action when learning a word		0.466		0.758
pVLS39	Grouping words together to study them		0.454		0.855
pVLS29	Taking notes when watching films and TV programmes		0.424		0.776
pVLS64	Practising with friends		0.423		0.843
pVLS2	Making word lists		0.415		0.724
pVLS52	Remembering words by remembering the situation/sentence in which it was used	0.365	0.405		0.796
pVLS8	Associating words with their position on page		0.396		0.742
pVLS18	Making word cards	− 0.337	0.390		0.672
pVLS10	Using rhyme to remember words		0.375		0.785

Table C.2 (*Continued*)

pVLS31	Writing down a word repeatedly		0.366	0.318	0.778
pVLS19	Looking for cognates		0.354		0.755
pVLS57	Associating words with synonyms or antonyms		0.337		0.650
pVLS46	Associating words with pictures and drawings		0.322		0.826
pVLS21	Remembering word if it is written down		0.303		0.671
pVLS23	Repeating new words aloud when studying			0.557	0.871
pVLS20	Planning for vocabulary learning		0.382	0.525	0.780
pVLS55	Getting help in conversations			0.507	0.719
pVLS3	Regular reviewing outside classroom			0.500	0.754
pVLS30	Asking someone for meaning			0.487	0.788
pVLS68	Reviewing before a test			− 0.463	0.707
pVLS59	Getting someone to test the knowledge			0.457	0.652
pVLS50	Defining words in the foreign language when testing oneself			0.443	0.824

Table C.2 (*Continued*)

pVLS12	Looking up words in bilingual dictionaries			0.432	0.735
pVLS44	Repeating words mentally			0.418	0.740
pVLS67	Testing oneself with word lists			0.416	0.825
pVLS14	Noting down new words in class			0.398	0.806
pVLS4	Testing oneself			0.398	0.783
pVLS65	Keeping a vocabulary notebook			0.372	0.742
pVLS37	Translating words into L1 to understand the meaning			0.359	0.696
pVLS32	Reading and leafing through a dictionary			0.342	0.765
pVLS49	Using spaced word practice			0.317	0.779
pVLS7	Asking the teacher to give the definition in the foreign language			0.316	0.709
pVLS15	Asking for correction			0.306	0.765
% of variance explained	11.233	6.134	4.991		
Cumulative%	11.233	17.368	22.359		
Cronbach's *a*	0.7851	0.8094	0.7720		

h^2, communality

Table C.3. Initial statistics for reduced pVLS items

Component	Eigenvalue	% Variance	Cumulative%
1	7.292	13.759	13.759
2	3.969	7.488	21.247
3	3.072	5.796	27.043
4	2.564	4.837	31.880
5	2.143	4.043	35.923
6	1.980	3.735	39.658
7	1.814	3.423	43.081
8	1.773	3.345	46.426
9	1.676	3.163	49.589
10	1.610	3.038	52.626
11	1.514	2.856	55.483
12	1.353	2.553	58.035
13	1.303	2.458	60.493
14	1.246	2.350	62.843
15	1.144	2.158	65.001
16	1.113	2.099	67.100
17	1.107	2.089	69.190
18	1.051	1.983	71.172
19	0.990	1.868	73.041
20	0.980	1.849	74.890
21	0.927	1.748	76.638
22	0.867	1.635	78.273
23	0.833	1.572	79.845
24	0.762	1.437	81.283
25	0.725	1.368	82.651
26	0.706	1.332	83.983

Table C.3 (*Continued*)

27	0.661	1.247	85.230
28	0.640	1.207	86.438
29	0.608	1.147	87.584
30	0.546	1.030	88.614
31	0.511	0.965	89.579
32	0.503	0.949	90.528
33	0.496	0.936	91.464
34	0.472	0.890	92.354
35	0.412	0.777	93.131
36	0.401	0.756	93.887
37	0.362	0.684	94.571
38	0.357	0.673	95.244
39	0.338	0.639	95.883
40	0.293	0.554	96.437
41	0.254	0.479	96.915
42	0.235	0.444	97.359
43	0.197	0.372	97.731
44	0.193	0.365	98.096
45	0.174	0.329	98.425
46	0.149	0.281	98.706
47	0.142	0.269	98.975
48	0.124	0.233	99.208
49	0.103	0.195	99.403
50	9.396×10^{-2}	0.177	99.580
51	8.200×10^{-2}	0.155	99.735
52	7.853×10^{-2}	0.148	99.883
53	6.198×10^{-2}	0.117	100.000

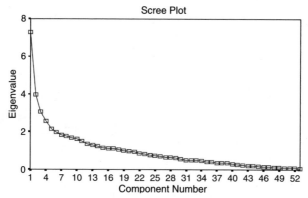

Figure C.2: Scree plot (initial reduced pVLS items)

Appendix D

Vocabulary Teaching Strategies:
Criteria and Results of Analyses

Table D.1: Criteria and results of lesson transcripts analysis (1 = VTS present)

id	Vocabulary teaching strategy	6th grade			7th grade			8th grade		
		T1	*T2*	*T3*	*T4*	*T5*	*T6*	*T7*	*T8*	*T9*
1	Affective strategy (encouragement, etc.)	1	1	1	1	1	1			1
2	Using board to									
2a	note words in FL		1	1	1	1	1	1	1	1
2b	display word cards	1	1	1	1	1				
2c	note translation into L1	1	1		1	1				
2d	graphically present relationships between words				1					
2e	note transcription						1			
2f	note collocations						1			
2g	note synonym or definition						1			
2h	note word class/ word forms									
2i	note word class	1		1			1	1		

Table D.1 (*Continued*)

3	Supplying additional information:										
3a	collocation						1				
3b	synonym or option		1		1	1	1				1
3c	similarities or differences	1	1	1			1				
3d	word class, grammar forms	1	1	1				1	1	1	1
3e	derivative	1	1					1			
3f	other meanings										
4	Games	1	1		1	1					1
5	Testing (oral/written) for evaluation			1					1	1	
5a	explanation in FL										
5b	translation from L1 into FL								1		
5c	translation from FL into L1								1	1	
5d	usage in a sentence										
5e	using a picture of a word										
5f	completing sentences with given words			1							
5g	guessing words from definitions										
6	Pronouncing words (presenting spoken form)	1		1	1	1	1	1	1		

Table D.1 (*Continued*)

7	Monitoring (of production):									
7a	correcting incorrect usage		1		1	1	1	1	1	1
7b	correcting incorrect pronunciation		1	1	1	1	1	1	1	1
7c	correcting incorrect *spelling*						1			
7d	asking for self-correction	1	1	1	1		1	1		
7e	asking for peer-correction	1		1	1		1	1		1
8	Monitoring (of comprehension)									
8a	asking directly	1	1	1	1	1	1	1	1	1
8b	confirming learners' translation	1	1	1	1	1	1	1	1	1
8c	translating into L1	1		1	1	1	1	1	1	1
8d	asking for synonym or option in L1	1		1	1					
9	Personalisation	1	1		1	1	1	1		1
10	Assistance (in retrieval)									
10a	giving antonyms		1		1					
10b	giving definitions				1		1			1
10c	giving hyponyms	1								
10d	contextualisation	1		1	1	1	1			1
10e	supplying the initial letter/ syllable		1				1	1	1	

Table D.1 (*Continued*)

10f	gesturing		1		1					
10g	giving word class				1	1				1
10h	reminding of word's location in textbook				1					
10i	using L1					1				1
11	Association with known words	1		1	1					
12	Association with experience, knowledge	1	1	1	1	1	1	1		1
	Presentation of meaning:									
13	using example sentences	1	1				1	1	1	1
14	using antonyms	1							1	
15	drawing on board		1							
16	definition in FL	1	1	1	1	1	1	1	1	1
17	explaining the context	1	1	1	1	1	1	1	1	1
18	translation into L1			1		1	1		1	1
19	supplying hyponyms	1		1	1					
20	gesturing				1	1				
21	pointing out word parts	1			1					
22	supplying synonyms			1	1	1	1	1	1	1
23	supplying taxonomic definition	1		1						
24	using pictures	1		1		1				

Table D.1 (*Continued*)

25	using realia									
26	Supplying the word in FL	1	1	1		1			1	1
	Strategic instructions (tips) for:									
27	importance of practising pronunciation	1								
28	paying attention to word forms			1						1
29	encouraging learners to ask for clarification			1	1	1	1	1		
30	vocabulary learning strategies									
31	pronouncing words mentally									
32	writing down words repeatedly									
33	noting down words while reading									
34	noting down words while watching TV									
35	reading extensively									
36	memorising word lists									
37	translating (in order to memorise words)									

Table D.1 (*Continued*)

38	regular revision at home										
39	listening to songs in FL										
40	looking for cognates										
41	using dictionaries					1			1		
42	imaging word's meaning										
43	imagining situa- tion/context										
44	Providing multiple encounters of words	1		1	1		1	1	1		
	Setting tasks:										
45	brainstorm		1		1		1				1
46a	make word cards										
46b	note words in notebooks	1		1	1	1		1	1		
46c	note words on board/ transparency	1	1	1			1				1
47	give antonyms		1								
48	give hyponyms										
49	give hyponyms		1	1	1		1	1			
50	give collocations						1				
51	give synonyms or options in FL	1	1	1	1		1	1	1		
52	give superordinates										
53	give word class		1				1	1	1		

Table D.1 (*Continued*)

54	complete sentences with given words		1	1	1	1	1	1		
55	complete the sentence with target word		1		1	1	1			
56	group words		1		1	1			1	
57	Setting task: identify words									
57a	find hyponyms									1
57b	find collocations									1
57c	find translation from L1 into FL							1		
57d	anagram		1							
57e	word puzzle etc.									1
57f	according to definitions									
58	Setting task: pronounce words/ read aloud	1	1	1	1	1	1	1	1	
58a	individually	1	1	1	1	1	1	1	1	
58b	in chorus	1					1	1		
	Setting tasks:									
59	memorise lists of words	1								
60	draw words									
61	explain the context		1							
62	give a definition in FL	1	1		1		1	1		
63	'act out' a word				1					

Table D.1 (*Continued*)

64	guess the word from gestures				1	1				
65	guess the word from associations	1	1		1	1				
66	guess the word from a definition		1		1			1	1	1
67	guess the word from the context							1		1
68	underline new words in the text	1	1	1	1					
69a	associate pictures with words (words not given)	1	1	1	1					
69b	associate real objects with words (words not given)	1								
70	translate into L1	1	1	1	1	1	1	1	1	1
71	translate into FL	1				1	1			
72	look up word in textbook, notebook etc.				1	1	1			
73	look up word's meaning in dictionaries								1	
74	Setting tasks: matching words									
74a	with definitions		1		1	1		1		1
74b	with collocations		1		1	1	1			
74c	with pictures	1	1	1						
74d	make compounds						1			

Table D.1 (*Continued*)

74e	with situation/ context		1		1					
74f	with related words/ derivatives									
74g	with synonyms									
74h	with antonyms									
74i	with translations									
75	Setting tasks: use words in sentences						1	1		1
76	Social strategies		1	1	1	1	1	1		1
76a	group work		1	1		1				1
76b	pair work		1		1		1	1		1
	Individual vocabulary teaching strategies (total)	45	50	42	54	44	53	37	30	39

Table D.2: Results of learning materials analysis (1 = teaching strategy present)

id	Teaching strategy	Learning materials					
		1	2	3	4	5	6
3c	Supplying additional information: similarities or differences						1
3e	Additional information: derivatives				1	1	1
3f	Information on other meanings					1	
4	Games	1	1	1	1	1	1
9	Personalisation	1	1	1	1	1	1

Table D.2 (*Continued*)

12	Association with experience, knowledge				1		1
	Presentation of meaning						
16	definition in FL	1	1	1	1		1
17	explaining the context	1		1	1		1
18	translation into L1	1					
24	using pictures	1	1	1			1
	Strategic instructions (tips) for:						
28	paying attention to word forms			1		1	
29	encouraging learners to ask for clarification			1	1	1	1
30	vocabulary learning strategies					1	
41	using dictionaries					1	
	Setting tasks:						
45	brainstorming	1	1	1	1	1	1
46a	make word cards		1				
46b	note words in notebook		1	1	1	1	1
47	give antonym		1	1	1	1	1
49	give hyponym				1		1
50	give collocation					1	1
51	give synonym or option in FL	1				1	
52	give superordinates					1	
53	give word class		1	1	1	1	1
54	complete sentences with given words	1	1	1	1	1	1
55	complete sentences with target word	1	1	1	1		1
56	group words	1	1	1	1	1	1
57	Setting task: identify words	1	1			1	
57a	find hyponyms	1		1			1

Table D.2 (*Continued*)

57b	find collocations			1	1		1
57d	anagram		1				
57e	word puzzle etc.	1	1	1	1	1	1
57f	according to definitions		1	1	1	1	1
58	Setting task: pronounce words/read aloud		1		1	1	1
	Setting tasks:						
59	memorise lists of words			1			
61	explain the context		1				
62	give a definition in FL		1		1		1
65	guess the word from associations	1	1	1			
66	guess the word from a definition		1	1	1		1
67	guess the word from the context		1	1	1	1	1
69a	associate pictures with words (words not given)	1		1		1	1
70	translate into L1	1	1	1	1		1
71	translate into FL				1		1
72	look up word in textbook, notebook etc.			1	1		1
73	look up word's meaning in dictionaries	1		1	1	1	1
74	Setting tasks: matching words	1				1	1
74a	with definitions	1	1	1	1	1	1
74b	with collocations	1	1	1	1	1	1
74c	with pictures	1	1	1	1	1	1
74d	make compounds			1			1

Table D.2 (*Continued*)

74e	with situation/context	1	1	1	1	1	1
74f	with related words/derivatives	1	1				1
74g	with synonyms	1	1		1	1	1
74h	with antonyms		1				
74i	with translations	1	1				
75	Setting tasks: use words in sentences	1	1	1	1	1	1
76	Social strategies	1	1	1	1		1
76a	group work	1	1	1			
76b	pair work	1	1	1	1		1
	Individual vocabulary teaching strategies (total):	30	35	35	34	31	42

1, Jagatić (1997); 2, Breka (2001); 3, Breka & Mardešić (2001); 4, Džeba & Mardešić (2001); 5, Mavar *et al.* (2000); 6, Jagatić (2000)

References

Abraham, R. and Vann, R. (1987) Strategies of two language learners: A case study. In A. Wenden and J. Rubin (eds) *Learner Strategies in Language Learning* (pp. 85–102). New York: Prentice Hall.

Ahmed, M.O. (1989) Vocabulary learning strategies. In P. Meara (ed.) *Beyond Words* (pp. 3–14). London: BAAL/CILT.

Aitchison, J. (1990) *Words In the Mind*. Oxford: Basil Blackwell.

Allen, V.F. (1983) *Techniques in Teaching Vocabulary*. Oxford: Oxford University Press.

Ančić, J. (2003) Strategije učenja kao važan faktor u usvajanju stranog jezika. In D. Stolac, N. Ivanetić and B. Pritchard (eds) *Psiholingvistika i kognitivna znanost u hrvatskoj primijenjenoj lingvistici* (pp. 1–8). Zagreb-Rijeka: HDPL Graftrade.

Anderson, J.R. (1995) *Learning and Memory: An Integrated Approach*. New York: Wiley.

Anderson, N. and Vandergrift, L. (1996) Increasing metacognitive awareness in the L2 classroom by using think-aloud protocols and other verbal report formats. In R. Oxford (ed.) *Language Learning Strategies Around the World: Cross-cultural Perspectives* (pp. 3–18). (Technical Report No. 13). University of Hawai'i, Second Language Teaching and Curriculum Center.

Atkinson, R. (1975) Mnemotechnics in second-language learning. *American Psychologist* 30, 821–828.

Atkinson, R.C. and Schiffrin, R.M. (1968) Human memory: A proposed system and its control processes. In K.W. Spence and J.T. Spence (eds) *The Psychology of Learning and Motivation* (pp. 89–105). New York: Academic Press.

Ausubel, D.P. (1967) Learning theory and classroom practice. *Bulletin, No. 1*. Toronto: Ontario Institute for Studies in Education.

Avila, E. and Sadoski, M. (1996) Exploring new applications of the keyword method to acquire English vocabulary. *Language Learning* 46 (Sept), 379–395.

Bachman, L.F. and Palmer, A.S. (1996) *Language Testing in Practice*. Oxford: Oxford University Press.

Baily, C.A. (1996) Unobtrusive computerized observation of compensation strategies for writing to determine the effectiveness of strategy instruction. In R. Oxford (ed.) *Language Learning Strategies Around the World: Cross-Cultural Perspectives* (pp. 141–150). (Technical Report No. 13). University of Hawai'i, Second Language Teaching and Curriculum Center.

Bedell, D. and Oxford, R. (1996) Cross-cultural comparisons of language learning strategies in the People's Republic of China and other countries. In R. Oxford (ed.) *Language Learning Strategies Around the World: Cross-cultural Perspectives* (pp. 47–60). (Technical Report No. 13). University of Hawai'i, Second Language Teaching and Curriculum Center.

Bellomo, T.S. (1999) Etymology of vocabulary development for the L2 college student. *TESL-EJ* 4 (2).

Bialystok, E. (1978) A theoretical model of second language learning. *Language Learning* 28 (1), 69–83.

Bialystok, E. (1979) The role of conscious strategies in second language proficiency. *Canadian Modern Language Review* 35, 372–394.

Bialystok, E. (1990) *Communication Strategies.* Oxford: Blackwell.

Bimmel, P. (1993) Lernstrategien im Deutschunterricht. *Fremdsprache Deutsch* 8 (1), 4–11.

Bosiljevac, H. (1996) Usvajanje vokabulara u nastavi engleskog jezika kao stranog. Unpublished MA Thesis, University of Zagreb.

Breka, O. (2001) *Way to Go 3* (textbook). Zagreb: Školska knjiga.

Breka, O. and Mardešić, M. (2001) *Way to Go 4* (textbook). Zagreb: Školska knjiga.

Bremner, S. (1999) Language learning strategies and language proficiency: Investigating the relationship in Hong Kong. *Canadian Modern Language Review* 55 (4), 490–514.

Brown, J.D. (2001) *Using Surveys in Language Programs.* Cambridge: Cambridge University Press.

Brown, C. and Payne, M.E. (1994) Five essential steps of processes in vocabulary learning. Paper presented at the TESOL Convention, Baltimore, MD.

Brown, T. and Perry, F. (1991) A comparison of three learning strategies for ESL vocabulary acquisition. *TESOL Quarterly* 25 (4), 655–670.

Carrell, P.L. (1989) Metacognitive awareness and second language reading. *Modern Language Journal* 73 (2), 121–134.

Carter, R. (1992) *Vocabulary: Applied Linguistic Perspectives.* London and New York: Routledge.

Chamot, A.U. (1987) The learning strategies of ESL students. In A. Wenden and J. Rubin (eds) *Learner Strategies in Language Learning* (pp. 71–83). New York: Prentice Hall.

Chamot, A.U. (2001) The role of learning strategies in second language acquisition. In M.P. Breen (ed.) *Learner Contributions to Language Learning* (pp. 25–43). Harlow, England: Longman.

Chin, C. (1999) The effects of three learning strategies on EFL vocabulary acquisition. *The Korea TESOL Journal* 2, 1–12.

Clahsen, H., Meisel, J. and Peinemann, M. (1983) *Deutsch als Zwietsprache: der Spracherwerb ausländischer Arbeiter.* Gunter Narr: Tübingen.

Coady, J. (2000) L2 vocabulary acquisition: A synthesis of the research. In J. Coady and T. Huckin (eds) *Second Language Vocabulary Acquisition: A Rationale for Pedagogy* (pp. 225–237). Cambridge: Cambridge University Press.

Cobb, T. (1997) Is there any measurable learning from hands-on concordancing? *System* 25 (3), 301–315.

Cohen, A. and Aphek, E. (1980) Retention of second-language vocabulary over time: investigating the role of mnemonic associations. *System* 8, 221–235.

Cohen, A. and Aphek, E. (1981) Easifying second language learning. *Studies in Second Language Acquisition* 3, 221–236.

Cohen, A.D. (1987) Studying learner strategies: How we get the information. In A. Wenden and J. Rubin (eds) *Learner Strategies in Language Learning* (pp. 57–69). New York: Prentice Hall.

Cohen, A.D. (1998) *Strategies in Learning and Using a Second Language.* New York: Addison Wesley Longman.

Cohen, A.D. and Scott, K. (1998) A synthesis of approaches to assessing language learning strategies. In A. Cohen (ed.) *Strategies in Learning and Using a Second Language* (pp. 26–49). New York: Addison Wesley Longman.

Cook, L.K. and Mayer, R.E. (1983) Reading strategies training for meaningful learning from prose. In M. Pressley and J. Levin (eds) *Cognitive Strategy Research* (pp. 83–131). New York: Springer Verlag.

Corder, S.P. (1967) The significance of learners' errors. *International Review of Applied Linguistics* 5, 161–170.

Dörnyei, Z. and Thurell, S. (1991) Strategic competence and how to teach it. *ELT Journal* 45 (1), 16–23.

Dreyer, C. and Oxford, R. (1996) Learning strategies and other predictors of ESL proficiency among Afrikaans speakers in South Africa. In R. Oxford (ed.) *Language Learning Strategies Around the World: Cross-Cultural Perspectives* (pp. 61–74). (Technical Report No. 13). University of Hawai'i, Second Language Teaching and Curriculum Center.

Džeba, B. and Mardešić, M. (2001) *Way to Go 5* (textbook). Zagreb: Školska knjiga.

Ehrman, M. and Oxford, R. (1989) Effects of sex differences, career choice, and psychological type on adult language learning strategies. *The Modern Language Journal* 73 (1), 1–13.

Ehrman, M. and Oxford, R. (1995) Cognition plus: Correlates of language learning success. *Modern Language Journal* 79 (1), 67–89.

Elbaum, B., Berg, C. and Dodd, D.H. (1993) Previous learning experience, strategy beliefs, and task definition in self-regulated foreign language learning. *Contemporary Educational Psychology* 18, 318–336.

Elhelou, M.A. (1994) Arab children's use of the keyword method to learn English vocabulary words. *Educational Research* 36 (3), 295–302.

Ellis, N.C. (1994) Consciousness in second language learning: Psychological perspectives on the role of conscious processes in vocabulary acquisition. *AILA Review* 11, 37–56.

Ellis, N.C. (1997) Vocabulary acquisition: Word structure, collocation, word-class, and meaning. In N. Schmitt and M. McCarthy (eds) *Vocabulary: Description, Acquisition and Pedagogy* (pp. 122–139). Cambridge: Cambridge University Press.

Ellis, N.C. and Beaton, A. (1995) Psycholinguistic determinants of foreign language vocabulary learning. In B. Harley (ed.) *Lexical Issues in Language Learning* (pp. 107–165). Amsterdam: Benjamins.

Ellis, R. (1995) *The Study of Second Language Acquisition.* Oxford: Oxford University Press.

Ellis, R. (2000) *Instructed Second Language Acquisition.* Oxford, UK and Cambridge, USA: Blackwell.

Ericson, K.A. (1988) Concurrent verbal reports on text comprehension: A review. *Text* 8, 295–325.

Færch, C. and Kasper, G. (1983) Procedural knowledge as a component of foreign language learners' communication Competence. In H. Boete and W. Herrlitz (eds) *Kommunikation im (Sprach-) Unterricth* (pp. 169–199). Utrecht: University of Utrecht.

Filipović, R. (1986) *Teorija jezika u kontaktu: uvod u lingvistiku jezičnih dodira.* Zagreb: JAZU/Školska knjiga.

Fox, J. (1984) Computer-assisted vocabulary learning. *ELT Journal* 38 (1), 27–33.

Fraser, C.A. (1999) Lexical processing strategy use and vocabulary learning through reading. *Studies In Second Language Acquisition (Special Issue)* 21 (2), 225–241.

Gagné, R.M. (1977) *The Conditions of Learning* (3rd edn). New York: Holt, Reinehart and Winston.

Gairns, R. and Redman, S. (1986) *Working With Words: A Guide to Teaching and Learning Vocabulary.* Cambridge: Cambridge University Press.

Gass, S. (1989) Second language vocabulary acquisition. *Annual Review of Applied Linguistics* 9, 92–106.

Gass, S. and Selinker, L. (2001) *Second Language Acquisition: An Introductory Course.* USA: Lawrence Erlbaum Associates.

Goh, C.M. (1998) How ESL learners with different listening abilities use comprehension strategies and tactics. *Language Teaching Research* 2 (2), 124–147.

Gonzalez, O. (1999) Building vocabulary: Dictionary consultation and the ESL student. *Journal of Adolescent and Adult Literacy* 43 (3), 264–270.

Graham, S. (1997) *Effective Language Learning: Positive Strategies for Advanced Level Language Learning.* Clevedon: Multilingual Matters.

Green, J.M. and Oxford, R. (1995) A closer look at learning strategies, L2 proficiency, and gender. *TESOL Quarterly* 29 (2), 261–297.

Griffin, G. and Harley, T.A. (1996) List learning of second language vocabulary. *Applied Psycholinguistics* 17 (4), 443–460.

Griffiths C. and Parr, J.M. (2001) Language learning strategies: Theory and perception. *ELT Journal* 55 (3), 247–254.

Gu, Y. and Johnson, R.K. (1996) Vocabulary learning strategies and language learning outcomes. *Language Learning* 46, 643–679.

Hair, J.E., Anderson, R.E., Tatham, R.L. and Black, W.C. (1998) *Multivariate Data Analysis.* New Jersey: Prentice Hall.

Halbach, A. (2000) Finding out about students' learning strategies by looking at their diaries: a case study. *System* 28, 85–96.

Harley, B. (2000) Listening strategies in ESL: Do age and L1 make a difference? *TESOL Quarterly* 34 (4), 769–777.

Hatch, E. and Brown, C. (2000) *Vocabulary, Semantics, and Language Education* (3rd printing). Cambridge: Cambridge University Press.

Henning, G.H. (1973) Remembering foreign language vocabulary: Acoustic and semantic parameters. *Language Learning* 23 (2), 185–196.

Hogben, D. and Lawson, M.J. (1994) Keyword and multiple elaboration strategies for vocabulary acquisition in foreign language learning (brief research report). *Contemporary Educational Psychology* 19, 367–376.

Hogben, D. and Lawson, M.J. (1997) Reexamining the relationship between verbal knowledge background and keyword training for vocabulary acquisition (brief research report). *Contemporary Educational Psychology* 22, 378–389.

Hosenfeld, C. (1984) Case studies of ninth grade readers. In J.C. Alderson and A.S. Urquhart (eds) *Reading in a Foreign Language.* (pp. 231–244). Harlow: Longman.

Hsiao, T. and Oxford, R. (2002) Comparing theories of language learning strategies: a confirmatory factor analysis. *The Modern Language Journal* 86 (3), 368–383.

Hulstijn, J. (2000) Mnemonic methods in foreign language vocabulary learning: Theoretical considerations and pedagogical implications. In J. Coady and T. Huckin (eds) *Second Language Vocabulary Acquisition* (pp. 203–224). Cambridge: Cambridge University Press.

Jagatić, M. (1997) *Speak English in Grade 6* (textbook). Zagreb: Školska knjiga.

Jagatić, M. (2000) *Speak English in Grade 8* (textbook). Zagreb: Profil.

Jenkins, J.R., Matlock, B. and Slocum, T.A. (1989) Two approaches to vocabulary instruction: the teaching of individual word meanings and practice in deriving word meanings from context. *Reading Research Quarterly* 24, 215–235.

Judd, E.L. (1978) Vocabulary teaching and TESOL: A need for reevaluation of existing assumptions. *TESOL Quarterly* 12 (1), 71–76.

Kang, S.-H. and Dennis, J.R. (1995) The effects of computer-enhanced vocabulary lessons on achievement of ESL grade school children. *Computer In the Schools* 11 (3), 25–35.

Kaplan, T.I. (1998) General learning strategies and the process of L2 acquisition: A critical overview. *IRAL* 36 (3), 233–246.

Kaylani, C. (1996) The influence of gender and motivation on EFL learning strategy use in Jordan. In R. Oxford (ed.) *Language Learning Strategies Around the World: Cross-Cultural Perspectives* (pp. 75–88). (Technical Report No. 13). University of Hawai'i, Second Language Teaching and Curriculum Center

Kojic-Sabo, I. and Lightbown, P. (1999) Students' approaches to vocabulary learning and their relationship to success. *The Modern Language Journal* 83 (2), 176–192.

Koolstra, C.M. and Beentjes, J.W.J. (1999) Children's vocabulary acquisition in a foreign language through watching subtitled television programs at home. *Educational Technology Research and Development* 47 (1), 51–60.

Koren, S. (1999) Vocabulary instruction through hypertext: Are there advantages over conventional methods of teaching? *TESL-EJ* 4 (1).

Krashen, S. (1981) *Second Language Acquisition and Second Language Learning.* Oxford: Pergamon Institute of English.

Kudo, Y. (1999) Second language vocabulary learning strategies. Second Language Teaching and Curriculum Center-On WWW at http://www.nflrc. hawaii.edu/networks/NW14/NW14.pdf. Accessed 14.4.02.

Kumaravadivelu, B. (1991) Language-learning tasks: Teacher intention and learner interpretation. *ELT Journal* 45 (2), 98–108.

Lamb, M. (2004) 'It depends on the students themselves': Independent language learning at an Indonesian state school. *Language, Culture and Curriculum* 17 (3), 229–245.

Lan, R. and Oxford, R. (2003) Language learning strategy profiles of elementary school students in Taiwan. *IRAL* 41, 339–379.

Laufer, B. (1986) Possible changes in attitude towards vocabulary acquisition research. *IRAL* XXIV (1), 69–75.

Laufer, B. (1991) The development of the L2 lexis in the expression of the advanced learner. *The Modern Language Journal* 75 (4), 440–448.

Laufer, B. (1997) What's in a word that makes it hard or easy: Some intralexical factors that affect learning of words. In N. Schmitt and M. McCarthy (eds)

Vocabulary: Description, Acquisition and Pedagogy (pp. 140–155). Cambridge: Cambridge University Press

Lawson, M.J. and Hogben, D. (1996) The vocabulary-learning strategies of foreign-language students. *Language Learning* 46, 101–135.

Lawson, M.J. and Hogben, D. (1998) Learning and recall of foreign-language vocabulary: Effects of a keyword strategy for immediate and delayed recall. *Learning and Instruction* 8 (2), 179–194.

Lessard-Clouston, M. (1996) ESL vocabulary learning in a TOEFL preparation class: A case study. *The Canadian Modern Language Review* 53 (1), 97–119.

Lessard-Clouston, M. (1997) Language learning strategies: An overview for L2 teachers. *The Internet TESL Journal III* 12. On WWW at http:/iteslj.org/Articles/Lessard-Clouston-Strategy.html. Accessed 14.4.02.

Lessard-Clouston, M. (1998) Vocabulary learning strategies for specialized vocabulary acquisition: A case study. Paper presented at the Annual Meeting of the Pacific Second Language Research Forum (3rd, Tokyo, Japan, 26 March 1998).

Levine, A. and Reves, T. (1998) Data collecting on reading-writing strategies: A comparison of instruments: A case study. *TESL-EJ* 3 (3).

Lewis, M. (1998) *Implementing the Lexical Approach: Putting Theory into Practice.* Hove: LTP Teacher Training.

Lewis, M. (2000a) (ed.) *Teaching Collocation: Further Developments in the Lexical Approach.* Hove: LTP Teacher Training.

Lewis, M. (2000b) There is nothing as practical as a good theory. In M. Lewis (ed.) *Teaching Collocation: Further Developments in the Lexical Approach* (pp. 10–27). Hove: LTP Teacher Training.

Liou, H. (2000) Assessing learner strategies using computers: New insights and limitations. *CALL* 13 (1), 65–78.

LoCastro, V. (1994) Learning strategies and learning environments. *TESOL Quarterly* 28 (2), 409–414.

LoCastro, V. (1995) The author responds [A response to Oxford and Green (1995)]. *TESOL Quarterly* 29 (1), 172–174.

Lucas, M.A. (1998) Language acquisition and the Conrad phenomenon. *IRAL* 36 (1), 69–82.

Luppescu, S. and Day, R.R. (1995) Reading, dictionaries, and vocabulary learning. In B. Harley (ed.) *Lexical Issues in Language Learning* (pp. 229–251). Amsterdam: Benjamins.

Matsumoto, K. (1996) Helping L2 learners reflect on classroom learning. *ELT Journal* 50 (2), 143–149.

Mavar, A., Crnić, S., Abbs, B., Freebairn, I. and Barker, C. (2000) *Snapshot* (textbook). Zagreb: VBZ.

McCarthy, M. (1994) *Vocabulary.* Oxford: Oxford University Press.

McCarthy, M. and Carter, R. (1997) Written and spoken vocabulary. In N. Schmitt and M. McCarthy (eds) *Vocabulary: Description, Acquisition and Pedagogy* (pp. 20–39). Cambridge: Cambridge University Press.

McDonough, S.H. (1995) *Strategy and Skill in Learning a Foreign Language.* London: Edward Arnold.

McLaughlin, B. (1987) *Theories of Second-Language Learning.* London, Baltimore, Melbourne, Auckland: Edward Arnold.

Meara, P. (1984) The study of lexis in interlanguage. In A. Davies, C. Criper and A.P.R. Howatt (eds) *Interlanguage* (pp. 25–35). Edinburgh: Edinburgh University Press.

Meara, P. (1997) Towards a new approach to modelling vocabulary acquisition. In N. Schmitt and M. McCarthy (eds) *Vocabulary: Description, Acquisition and Pedagogy* (pp. 109–121). Cambridge: Cambridge University Press.

Melka, F. (1997) Receptive vs. productive aspects of vocabulary. In N. Schmitt and M. McCarthy (eds) *Vocabulary: Description, Acquisition and Pedagogy* (pp. 84–102). Cambridge: Cambridge University Press.

Merrifield, J. (1997) *Examining the Language Learning Strategies Used by French Adult Learners*. Birmingham, UK: Aston University.

Mihaljević Djigunović, J. (1999) Kako motivirani učenici uče strani jezik? *Strani jezici* XXVIII (3–4), 191–196.

Mihaljević Djigunović, J. (2000) Language learning strategies and affect. *CLCS Occasional Paper No.59*, Trinity College, Dublin.

Moon, R. (1997) Vocabulary connections: Multi-word items in English. In N. Schmitt and M. McCarthy (eds) *Vocabulary: Description, Acquisition and Pedagogy* (pp. 40–63). Cambridge: Cambridge University Press.

Morgan, J. and Rinvolucri, M. (1986) *Vocabulary.* Oxford: Oxford University Press.

Nagy, W. (1997) On the role of context in first- and second-language vocabulary learning. In N. Schmitt and M. McCarthy (eds) *Vocabulary: Description, Acquisition and Pedagogy* (pp. 64–83). Cambridge: Cambridge University Press.

Naiman, N., Frohlich, M., Stern, H.H. and Todesco, A. (1978) *The Good Language Learner*. Research in Education Series 7. Toronto: Ontario Institute for Studies in Education Press.

Nation, I.S.P. (1990) *Teaching and Learning Vocabulary.* New York: Newbury House.

Nation, I.S.P. (2001) *Learning Vocabulary in Another Language*. Cambridge: Cambridge University Press.

Nemser, W. (1971) Approximative systems of foreign language learners. *IRAL 9*, 115–23.

Nyikos, M. and Oxford, R. (1993) A factor analytic study of language-learning strategy use: Interpretations from information-processing theory and social psychology. *The Modern Language Journal* 77 (II), 11–22.

O'Gorman, E. (1996) An investigation of the mental lexicon of second language learners. *Teanga: the Irish Yearbook of Applied Linguistics* 16, 15–31.

O'Malley, M.J. (1987) The effects of training in the use of learning strategies on acquiring English as a second language. In A. Wenden and J. Rubin (eds) *Learner Strategies in Language Learning* (pp. 133–144). New York: Prentice Hall.

O'Malley, M.J. and Chamot, A.U. (1996) *Learning Strategies in Second Language Acquisition*. Cambridge: Cambridge Applied Linguistics.

O'Malley, J.M., Chamot, A.U., Stewner-Manzanares, G., Küpper, L. and Russo, R. (1985a) Learning strategies used by beginning and intermediate ESL students. *Language Learning* 35 (1), 21–46.

O'Malley, J.M., Chamot, A.U., Stewner-Manzanares, G., Russo, R. and Küpper, L. (1985b) Learning strategy application with students of ESL. *TESOL Quarterly* 19 (3), 557–584.

Onwuegbuzie, A., Bailey, P. and Daley, C.E. (2000) Cognitive, affective, personality, and demographic predictors of foreign language achievement. *Journal of Educational Research* 94 (1), 3–15.

Oxford, R. (1990) *Language Learning Strategies: What Every Teacher Should Know.* Boston: Heinle & Heinle.

Oxford, R. (1992/3) Language learning strategies in a nutshell: Update and ESL suggestions. *TESOL Journal* 2 (2), 18–22.

Oxford, R. (ed.) (1996) *Language Learning Strategies Around the World: Cross-Cultural Perspectives* (Technical Report No. 13). University of Hawai'i, Second Language Teaching and Curriculum Center

Oxford, R. and Ehrman, M. (1993) Second language research on individual differences. *Annual Review of Applied Linguistics* 13, 188–205.

Oxford, R. and Scarcella, R.C. (1994) Second language vocabulary learning among adults: State of the art in vocabulary instruction. *System* 22 (2), 231–243.

Oxford, R., Lavine, R.Z., Felkins, G., Hollaway, M.E. and Saleh, A. (1996) Telling their stories: Language students use diaries and recollection. In R. Oxford (ed.) *Language Learning Strategies Around the World: Cross-Cultural Perspectives.* (Technical Report No. 13) (pp. 19–34). University of Hawai'i, Second Language Teaching and Curriculum Center.

Oxford, R., Cho, Y., Leung, S. and Kim, H. (2004) Effect of the presence and difficulty of task on strategy use: An exploratory study. *IRAL* 42, 1–47.

Pallant, J. (2001) *SPSS Survival Manual.* Buckingham, Philadelphia: Open University Press.

Palmberg, R. (1988) Computer games and foreign language vocabulary learning. *ELT Journal* 42 (4), 247–252.

Pavičić, V. (1999) Model strateškog pristupa učenju vokabulara engleskog jezika. *Strani jezici* XXVIII (3–4), 209–217.

Pavičić, V. (2000) Istraživanje strategija učenja vokabulara. *Strani jezici* XXIX (1–2), 15–26.

Pawling, E. (1999) Modern languages and CD-ROM-based learning. *British Journal of Educational Technology* 30 (2), 163–175.

Peacock, M. and Ho, B. (2003) Student language learning strategies across eight disciplines. *International Journal of Applied Linguistics* 13 (2), 179–200.

Pearson, E. (1988) Learner strategies and learner interviews. *ELT Journal* 42 (3), 173–178.

Politzer, R.L. and McGroarty, M. (1985) An exploratory study of learning behaviors and their relationships to gains n linguistic and communicative competence. *TESOL Quarterly* 19, 103–123.

Porte, G. (1988) Poor language learners and their strategies for dealing with new vocabulary. *ELT Journal* 42 (3), 167–172.

Pressley, M., Levin, J.R., Kuiper, N.A., Bryant, S.L. and Michene, S. (1982) Mnemonic versus nonmnemonic vocabulary-learning strategies: Additional comparisons. *Journal of Educational Psychology* 74, 693–707.

Prince, P. (1996) Second language vocabulary learning: The role of context versus translation as a function of proficiency. *The Modern Language Journal* 80 (4), 478–493.

Purpura, J.E. (1994) The role of learner strategies in language learning and testing. Paper given at the Thai TESOL Conference, Bangkok, January, 1994.

Purpura, J. (1999) *Learner Strategy Use and Performance on Language Tests. A Structural Equation Modelling Approach.* (University of Cambridge Local Examinations Syndicate). Studies in Language Testing 8.

Qian, D. (1996) ESL vocabulary acquisition: contextualization and decontextualization. *Canadian Modern Language Review* 53, 120–142.

Reiss, M. (1985) The good language learner: Another look. *The Canadian Modern Language Review* 41 (3), 511–523.

Ridley, J. (1997) *Reflection and Strategies in Foreign Language Learning*. Frankfurt am Main: Lang.

Ringbom, H. (1987) *The Role of the First Language in Foreign Language Learning*. Philadelphia: Multilingual Matters Ltd.

Rivers, W. (1981) *Teaching Foreign Language Skills*. Chicago, London: The University of Chicago Press.

Robinson, P. (ed.) (2001) *Cognition and Second Language Instruction*. Cambridge: Cambridge University Press.

Rodriguez, M. and Sadoski, M. (2000) Effects of rote, context, keyword, and context/keyword methods on retention of vocabulary in EFL classrooms. *Language Learning* 50 (2), 385–412.

Rubin, J. (1975) What the 'good language learner' can teach us. *TESOL Quarterly* 9 (1), 41–51.

Rubin, J. (1987) Learner strategies: Theoretical assumptions, research history and typology. In A. Wenden and J. Rubin (eds) *Learner Strategies in Language Learning* (pp. 15–30). New York: Prentice Hall.

Sagarra, N. and Alba, M. (2006) The key is in the keyword: L2 vocabulary learning methods with beginning learners of Spanish. *The Modern Language Journal* 90 (ii), 228–243.

Sanaoui, R. (1995) Adult learners' approach to learning vocabulary in second languages. *Modern Language Journal* 79 (1), 15–28.

Sawyer, M. and Ranta, L. (2001) Aptitude, individual differences, and instructional design. In P. Robinson (ed.) *Cognition and Second Language Instruction* (pp. 319–353). Cambridge: Cambridge University Press.

Schmitt, N. (1997) Vocabulary learning strategies. In N. Schmitt, and M. McCarthy (eds) *Vocabulary: Description, Acquisition and Pedagogy* (pp. 198–227). Cambridge: Cambridge University Press.

Schmitt, N. (2000) *Vocabulary in Language Teaching*. Cambridge: Cambridge Language Education.

Schmitt, N. and Schmitt, D. (1993) Identifying and assessing vocabulary learning strategies. *Thai TESOL Bulletin* 5 (4), 27–33.

Schmitt, N. and Schmitt, D. (1995) Vocabulary notebooks: Theoretical underpinnings and practical suggestions. *ELT Journal* 49 (2), 133–143.

Schmidt, R. (2001) Attention. In P. Robinson (ed.) *Cognition and Second Language Instruction* (pp. 3–32). Cambridge: Cambridge University Press.

Schneider, V.I., Healy, A.F. and Bourne, L.E. Jr. (2002) What is learned under difficult conditions is hard to forget: Contextual interference effects in foreign vocabulary acquisition, retention and transfer. *Journal of Memory and Language* 46, 419–440.

Seal, B. (1991) Vocabulary learning and teaching. In M. Celce-Murcia (ed.) *Teaching English as a Foreign or Second Language* (2nd edn) (pp. 296–312). New York: Newbury House.

Segler, T.M., Pain, H. and Sorace, A. (2001) Second language vocabulary acquisition and learning strategies in ICALL environments. Submitted to

Workshop on CALL, AI-Ed 2001 (San Antonio, TX). On WWW at http:/homepages.inf.ed.ac.uk/s9808690/finalpaper2.pdf. Accessed 21.2.06.

Selinker, L. (1972) Interlanguage. *IRAL* 10 (2), 209–231.

Selinker, L., Baumgartner-Cohen, B., Kinahan, C. and Mathieu, E. (2000) Researching learning strategies in second language acquisition. In M. Dakowska (ed.) *English in the Modern World*. Festschrift for Hartmut Breitkreuz on the Occasion of his Sixtieth Birthday. (FLS. Foreign Language Studies 5) (pp. 19–25). Frankfurt am Main: Peter Lang.

Singleton, D. (1999) *Exploring the Second Language Mental Lexicon*. Cambridge: Cambridge University Press.

Skehan, P. (2000) *A Cognitive Approach to Language Learning*. Oxford: Oxford University Press.

Škiljan, D. (1994) *Pogled u lingvistiku*. Rijeka: Naklada Benja.

Sökmen, A.J. (1997) Current trends in teaching second language vocabulary. In N. Schmitt, and M. McCarthy (eds) *Vocabulary: Description, Acquisition and Pedagogy* (pp. 237–257). Cambridge: Cambridge University Press.

Stern, H.H. (1975) 'What can we learn from the good language learner?' *Canadian Modern Language Review* 31, 304–318.

Stern, H.H. (1986) *Fundamental Concepts of Language Teaching*. Oxford: Oxford University Press.

Sternberg, R.J. (1987) Most vocabulary is learned from context. In M.G. McKeown and M.E. Curtis (eds) *The Nature of Vocabulary Acquisition* (pp. 89–105). Hillsdale, NJ: Erlbaum.

Stevick, E.W. (1996) *Memory, Meaning, and Method: Some Psychological Perspectives on Language Learning*. Boston: Heinle and Heinle.

Stoffer, I. (1995) University foreign language students' choice of vocabulary learning strategies as related to individual difference variables. Unpublished PhD Dissertation, University of Alabama.

Swan, M. (1997) The influence of the mother tongue on second language vocabulary acquisition and use. In N. Schmitt and M. McCarthy (eds) *Vocabulary: Description, Acquisition and Pedagogy* (pp. 156–180). Cambridge: Cambridge University Press.

Tarone, E. (1981) Some thoughts on the notion of communication strategy. *TESOL Quarterly* 15 (3), 285–295.

Thatcher, P. (2000) Acquisition and learning – theory matters. *IRAL* 38 (2), 161–174.

Thompson, I. (1987) Memory in language learning. In A. Wenden and J. Rubin (eds) *Learner Strategies in Language Learning* (pp. 43–56). New York: Prentice Hall.

Thornbury, S. (2002) *How to Teach Vocabulary*. Harlow: Longman.

Tsou, W., Wang, W. and Li, H. (2002) How computers facilitate English foreign language learners acquire English abstract words. *Computers and Education* 39 (4), 415–428.

Vandergrift, L. (1995) Language learning strategy research: Development of definitions and theory. *Journal of the CAAL* 17 (1), 87–104.

Wakamoto, N. (2000) Language learning strategy and personality variables: Focusing on extroversion and introversion. *IRAL* 38 (1), 71–81.

Weaver, S. and Cohen, A. (1997) *Strategies Based Instruction: A Teacher Training Manual.* Center for Advanced Research in Language Acquisition, University of Minnesota Working Papers series 7.

Weinstein, C.E. and Mayer, R.E. (1986) The teaching of learning strategies. In M.C. Wittrock (ed.) *Handbook of Research on Teaching* (pp. 315–327). New York: Macmillan.

Wenden, A. (1987) Conceptual background and utility. In A. Wenden and J. Rubin (eds) *Learner Strategies in Language Learning* (pp. 3–14). New York: Prentice Hall.

Wenden, A. (1991) *Learner Strategies for Learner Autonomy.* New York: Prentice Hall.

Wenden, A. (2001) Metacognitive knowledge in SLA: The neglected variable. In M.P. Breen (ed.) *Learner Contributions To Language Learning* (pp. 44–64). Harlow, England: Longman.

Wharton, G. (2000) Language learning strategy use of bilingual foreign language learners in Singapore. *Language Learning*, 50 (2), 203–244.

Williams, M. and Burden, R.L. (2001) *Psychology for Language Teachers.* Cambridge: Cambridge University Press.

Wong, M.S.L. (2005) Language learning strategies and language self-efficacy: Investigating the relationship in Malaysia. *RELC* 36 (3), 245–269.

Young, R. and Perkins, K. (1995) Cognition and conation in second language acquisition theory. *IRAL* 33 (2), 142–164.

Zarevski, P. (1994) *Psihologija pamćenja i učenja.* Jastrebarsko: Naklada Slap.

Zhang, Z. and Schumm, J. (2000) Exploring effects of the keyword method on limited English proficient students' vocabulary recall and comprehension. *Reading Research and Instruction* 39 (3), 202–221.

Index